Divine Creation

❧ Lucy ❦

Cover design and layout: Dalit Rahamim
Author's image: Zvika Goldstein
Book's cover photo and Illustrations: Pixabay.com, Just color.net

1st edition 2016, 2nd edition 2018 © All rights reserved to:

Lucy, Medium

Remote channeling sessions

www.lucy4you.com

ISBN: 978-1-61984-487-2

Divine Creation

Lucy

&ó Contents &ó

๛ *Divine Message* ๏ 1 ๛

"*All of you shall care for one another and be as one and*

I shall gather you from the four corners of the world.

I shall uplift your souls from the gutters, to lead you from despa

and doom with the ancient knowledge to ' Tikkun Olam'

reforming world order.

Righteousness and purity shall cleanse your thirsty souls,

to prepare you for the future, teach you the secrets and **unite**

your souls.

In the distant future, I shall wash your faces in a turbulent

ocean, earthquakes, and signs.

This book is for the generations, contain my words.

There is no anger, fury or punishment - all of me is love."

๛ This message was received through channeling ๛

๛๏๛

I prayed to God: "Let me have everything so that I may enjoy life".

& God replied: "I gave you life - so that you may enjoy everything".

A folk sayin

❧ Divine Message ☯ 2 ❧

Dearly beloved,

Who is asking for assistance and guidance in your life,

so you may understand where you should turn to next

Go to the wise and silent person,

who does not ask for alms or provides you with talismans,

who does not walk in wearing fine clothes

or spends his time in temples and luxurious buildings.

You will reach that person by word of mouth.

Be wise, go to the modest, quiet, and humble ones.

The words of wisdom of heaven are spoken quietly

with humor and a smile, not with shouting, threats

and intimidation.

Not by might nor by power,

but by spirit, I am the LORD.

❧ This message was received through channeling ❧

❧ Introduction ❦

This book was written using male pronouns, yet it is intended to apply to both genders.

I would like to thank all those who purchased, received or borrowed this book. Nothing is coincidental!
This book was meant to fall into your hands.

All that is required of you, the reader, is curiosity, flexible thinking, a willingness to accept new ideas with an open mind and a healthy sense of humor. This book was written to satisfy the public's interest and curiosity in the insights and knowledge I speak so often about.

I gather all of the knowledge, insights, and messages that my soul has collected in its thousands of incarnations. This book was dictated to me at night through channeling within two months, first in Hebrew and then translated into English. It was intuitively and directly typed into the computer.

The book's contents explanations in simple and humorous language to the question "Who are we?" as well as other important questions, such as:

- Who are God /'The Creation' , 'The Creators', and 'The Created' ?

- How was life on Earth and humanity created ?

- Why are we here and what is the purpose of humanity in the universe?

- What are fate, destiny and soul?

- What are heaven and hell, and is there life after death?

- How are the biblical era and the era of the dinosaurs connected?

- What are the rules of the universe?

Before we begin, here are few basic insights:

1. There never was and never will be a single truth.

For one simple reason: it denies the right to choose. If there was only one truth – you would have been prevented from thinking otherwise. Therefore, accept the contents of this book as an additional opinion that can enrich the knowledge you already possess. It is important that you form your own personal opinion and way of thinking. Open your mind and never blindly follow other people's ideas.

2. You are all temporary guests on any earth.

Nothing was or will be yours forever, other than your free will. Even your soul is not yours! it belongs to *'The Creation'* / God !
Life is like a game of monopoly: Each player (a human being) begins at the starting point (birth) with a backpack (the journey of the soul) and a roadmap (the lines of destiny) which were chosen in advance to be experienced in a physical human form by the player during his life.

During this game, the player undergoes changes, buys/sel
builds/separates,

ascend/descends, finishes the game's round (dies) and
returns to the starting point and then starts all over again
(the soul reborn in a new body or stay as a spirit) with a ne
roadmap (the lines of destiny) in a new location somewher
on Earth or in some other location in the infinite universe.

❧ Your aim is to recreate endlessly.

You are all originally - souls of spirit. You choose to be
embodied in living bodies (material) for a short time in ord
to testify the nature of:

> *1.)* who you are as a spirit.
> *2.)* The nature of *The Creation or God's spirit.*

❧ God can never be ONE entity

The universe always allows a free choice between at least
two options, that's why God is not one entity but several.

❧ No material will make spirit happy for long, but emotions will.

⮞ You cannot die.

You are made of spirit which cannot be extinguished. You're all eternal souls.

⮞ "All is foreseen, but freedom of choice is given".

A question may occur:

" If all is foreseen - then where is the person's selection?"

So the answer is:

" The Creation / God will never interfere in the human's choice. A divine pattern exists with the main destiny lines of each person while there is free will to select each move and decisions."

For example: Driving a vehicle on an existing road that has multiple paths (= all is foreseen) yet **the right to choose how and where to drive** between those paths through interchanges and shortcuts is given to you, the driver (= freedom of choice is given).

You can lengthen or shorten the path, but eventually, you will reach the same target foretold. All will happen - only time changes.

ಞ All the diseases originate from the soul.

A spirit cannot be cured using only material; therefore, medicines (drugs) can't cure - but only can silence the problem which stems from the person's soul.

In order to truly heal - you must combine the work of a doctor with a diagnosis of a medium and treatment from a healer.

The astrological sign of the Zodiac contains the order of the 12 Ages, which affects the ten planets surrounding the sun in the Milky Way Galaxy, including Earth. The only planet on which life can exist.

ಞ In every Galaxy, life can exist only on one planet!

Therefore, of the nine planets in the solar system,

life can exist only on planet Earth.

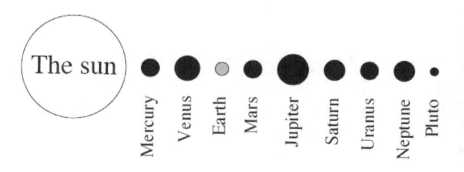

❧ All religions involve material and violate the free will.

Spirituality cannot be religious because a spirit is the opposite of corporeality.

A religious man:

Deals with a material: houses of worship, books, talismans, ceremonies, religious artifacts, and clothing.

A spirit man:

Does not deal with religion or material but communicate with *The Creation* without many additional accessories, modestly and quietly without dictating.

❧ You do not need any mediators.

All of you are associated with *The Creation / God* once you have been created. You are all an infinite spirit with a soul that lent to you for your journey in a tangible body.

❧ The humankind on Earth was created by the Creators =

the Extra-terrestrial, while planet Earth serves as an experimental lab. (Additional information is in my book: 'Divine Creation'/2016).

Jesus (Joshua) was sent by *The Creation* to Earth to undo t
religions and open a new Age without religions and materi
slavery, but absurdly and unintentional Jesus created the
religion of Christianity.

The enormous absurd is: the establishment of the Christian
religion "state" of the Vatican in Rome under the Pope, wh(
it's known that the Romans crucified and killed Jesus.

The three main religions: Christianity, Judaism, and Islam
expanded & were blown out of proportion, using extreme
control, threats and intimidations **by dictating** to their
followers:

- Arrival to prayer complexes and religious classes, setting
  dates of holidays and ceremonies, prohibited of mixing
  between believers from different religions; especially
  when it comes to marriage or burial then it gets more
  absurd.

- Marriage ceremonies that unite only those who believe ir
  the same religion or burial ceremonies that
allow only to their believers to be buried on 'their land'.

- By dictating to their believers what and when to eat, on
  which days to strike and fast.

- Receiving donations up to an establishment of cults or
  radical factions.

All religions work in the form of unnecessary mediation agencies between humans and *The Creation / God* while they have been funded by governments, public and generation of believers.

Between all religions there is a consistent marketing competition that promises to unite their believers and transform them to a 'better people' by giving them answers from the "holy" books, which mostly contain tales from ancient times, remember:

Any <u>Material</u> will never be holy - except for <u>Souls</u>.

This industrial-religion is rolling a tons of money for generations by exploitation and servitude their believers with no option to innovation, with **the goal of turning their believers into slaves in 'the name of God'.**
Human beings have an ego; therefore, religions will not be able to exist in peace.

Historical evidence: **Religions never have united <u>but divided and dispersed hatred</u>** up to the extinction of all that is different and unfortunately, it's also relevant even today.

Every religion revolves and violates human freedom.
Religions are not spirituality.

- **A religion man**: dictates without choice and dealing with materials such as houses of worship, ceremonies, cemeteries, books, laws and rules, artifacts and clothing.

- **A spiritual man**: provides a free choice; therefore, he isn't religion and does not deal with the material but communicates with *The Creation spirit* without any aid.

෭෨෪

You do not need mediators, you are all associated with God and *The Creation* from the moment of your creation and all of you have an infinite soul that has been lent to you.

God is not in the religions - but in the spirit of faith.

God did not create religions or time - humanity did.

God can never be One - It against freedom of choice.

There are no religions in the universe,

but free will & faith.

The universe's purpose: humanity was created by **The Creator** (the extra-terrestrial /aliens) on planet Earth which is used as an experimental laboratory in order to continue *The Creation's engine.*

By the creation of human beings who will create other human beings in a circular manner, like on other planets on which life takes place.

You are a soul (spirit) which embodied in a human body (material) **to indicate the nature of you - as a spirit**, in order to **indicate the nature of** *The Creation / God*.
(Divine Creation, Lucy/2016).

There is no Material that can make a spirit (soul) happy for a long time, only emotions are associated with happiness of the soul; Therefore, all diseases are affected first from the soul and secondly from the physical body. **You cannot cure the soul (spirit) only by using material;** drugs cannot cure – but only create a temporary silence.

- As I wrote in the book The Future', from the year 2106 religions will be replaced by free faith:
   "In the universe, there are no religions but faith."

- As higher levels of education will be increased – religion will decrease.

Remember:

Life can exist only on one planet in each galaxy.

The tool for understanding the universe is the international language of: The mathematics.

❧ About me ❧

I was born and grew up in Israel. As a child, my parents were busy providing and I had a great deal of quality time by myself with an active imagination, patience with fearless of experiencing new things. I noticed that when I asked a question - then a reply immediately popped into my mind and I got information and visual vision from an inner voice who keeps talking to me until today.

At the time, I thought that my experiences were typical to all children, but over the years I discovered that I'm the weird one who is exceptional. Out of boredom and loneliness, I opened up to the world of the spirit, there I felt protected and there was no one to stop me or doubt my inner world. At the age of six, I began to hear & see beyond and have conversations with deceased relatives.

There I received that my real destiny is: to transfer messages and insights, especially while the humanity is entering the Aquarius Age during my lifetime; therefore, the humanity and technologies are highly changing rapidly to the benefit of the planet Earth and all humanity on it.

Life is a play: Earth serves as a theatrical stage upon it humanity appears in changing sets, costumes, roles, languages, customs, culture, and progress.

I have always been fascinated by the spiritual world that is hidden from sight. In my professional, I am a practical architectural engineer but more than that I'm a spiritual woman, a medium since the age of six (a descendant of Rabbi Haim Ben-Atar). I am non-religious Jewish but **full of endless faith** in *God, The Creation,* and *The Creators* **because religion contradicts the human freedom of choice.** I serve as a vessel for passing through messages. **I am an ancient soul** who came to Earth with enormous knowledge & ability to communicate with the spirits world.

The moment a person acts according to rules and regulations that were written by others and not according to his own choice, **this person is blocking himself from personal experience and creating his own negative** *karma.*

Religion goes against the human freedom of choice.

In the universe there is **no religion – but only faith.**

It is the inner faith that makes the difference

and not the external appearance.

In every aspect of life,

the moment you ask 'why' and

do not receive a logical answer,

it is the time to stop and rethink the matter.

How do I channeling and communicate with entities:

I receive communications and messages through thoughts into my right head.. and no, I do not hear voices.

I simply close my eyes and see a vision filled with details and images. I listen and pass on the messages and answers filled with information from the spiritual world.

The ability to channel can be illustrated in this way: there are many drivers on the roads.

Mediums are:

- Much like race car drivers, there aren't many of them and they are very fast.

- Mediums use most of their ten senses so, their intuition sense is highly developed.

- Mediums are very curious and constantly seek new experiences and do not fear the unknown, if everything is known so there is nothing to fear.

"*Around the world*
people pay their respects
to glorify religious leaders
clothed in various outfits.

Which are portrayed as more reliable and trust
than true people of the spirit,
such as mystics and mediums
who are portrayed as strange or charlatans.

Person's outward appearance and clothing
do not indicate his quality, integrity,
reliability and true personality."

Mystical events in my life

Realization of destiny

During my twenties, after many years of working as practical architecture, I decided to quit my job after receiving an inner message: *"My dear, it is time for you to go The department is about to close down. This is the right time for you to begin fulfilling your true destiny."* I shared this message with my manager, but despite his lack of faith a short time after I left - my prediction came true!   This incident strengthened my sense of confidence to fulfill my destiny - working as a medium.

A messenger

I entered a restaurant and noticed an old man in tattered clothes look at the restaurant's window, it felt as only I saw him. I went outside and put some money in his hand; he returned it back and said: *"I don't want your money, I want to eat."* He refused to come inside and stayed on the sidewalk. bought him a meal, went outside and gave it to him. He didn't say anything just kissed my palm and took the food. On my way back inside I turned back to, but he vanished! He was a messenger who sent from above to test me.

Encounter with extraterrestrial (Aliens)

One night I woke up and felt my entire body paralyzed except blinking my eyes. I saw two aliens standing in front of me, looking at me. Their appearance was: height around one and a half feet, head shaped like an upturned pear, eyes large and cat-like, no eyelashes or body hair, small mouths, and noses. I wasn't afraid and began to communicate with them through telepathy: *"Why did it take you so long to come? I've been waiting for you since an early age."* and they responded: *"We've been here all the time; **you are the one who wasn't ready for us.**"*

I remembered from that encounter how my body rose in the air and with a single blink they rotated me as I was floating in the air so that I faced the floor and were led through my room's open window to around spaceship covered with small illuminated windows with unusual structure of links that make up the spaceship's floor. I received some kind of treatment in the spaceship, but they erased my memory. In that same night, I received the ability to see X-rays even remotely. In the following day, I woke up extremely tired.

Over the years up to these days, I continue to communicate with them and receive treatment from them.

Trip to London

I went with a friend to London. We took a ferry at the river Thames. During that cruise, I closed my eyes and saw a vision: *'the entire city of London is on fire'*. A few weeks later I discover about 'The Great Fire of London' that broke out in the year 1666. There is no coincidence.

As we were celebrating my birthday, we went into a big toy store on Oxford Street. My friend announced to one of the salesmen that I'm a medium, he insisted to receive a personal message, so I told him: *"You were here in London at the age of 17 on a family trip with your parents and your little sister"*, he was stunned: *"It's true! how did you know that? I will gather the rest of the employees, please come to the fifth floor"*. Without requesting it, I found myself on the fifth floor channeling for the store's employees. In one special case, one manager approached me so I asked him: *"Why are you sad? Your sister is already feeling better after her operation"* He was surprised and told me that his sister had undergone heart surgery. I began to see her heart from afar, using an 'x-ray vision': *"The source of your sister's heart condition was the lower left valve, which separates the chambers of the heart, it did not function properly and the problem was fixed following that operation"*. He immediately called his mother which verified all the details I gave him!

After four hours we came out of the store. While we were standing on Oxford Street, I told my friend to look at the sky: *"The Creation is sending us a message and a hug from above."* Then after two minutes an airplane emerged and marked a white stripe in the sky.

The woman in black

One morning, a seventy years old woman came to a channeling session. She wore a black dress; her hair was black and disheveled. She sat in front of me and began to complain how *"mystics have ruined her life by 'not allowing' her to ever experience love or marriage"*. I felt her negative energy and noticed a satanic male entity dwelled within her, so I immediately protected myself and asked that entity: *"What have you come to me seeking? What is it that you want? I am protected, you cannot harm me."*

The woman continued complaining and began to curse; I opened the door and asked her to leave. An hour later I smelled something burning in the room and when I rose my head up I saw a "fiery flame" erupting from the top of my head. I put out the fire; some burnt pieces of paper fell down but amazingly my hair and scalp were not damaged.

I received a message: *"What you have now experienced was sent to you by the woman in black".*
I pressed my palms together & sent that same energy back to her and I asked for *The Creation* to let justice be done.

Out of body experience

One night I woke up from my sleep paralyzed without the ability to move besides my eyes. On the wall in front of me saw a wide camera film open up and in it three picture frames. Paralyzed I saw myself in a form of a hovering whi dove, flies between several images from my previous incarnations. My soul rose out of my chest and entered into the first picture frame. This process repeated itself three times. In each frame I saw myself in different places, speaking a different language until the whole process ended Moments later a spiral white light appeared in front of me and it began to turn in a circle, while tiny chubby color angels, without any sexual identity, were flying around the spiral and heavenly music of harp was in the background. Wow! That was a divine experience!

The prince of darkness

I borrowed a spiritual book and read the first half. The following day, while reading the second half, I realized that the contents were not as "enlightened" as I had thought. I saw it as a moral obligation to note this in my first book. At midnight I placed the book on the nightstand and sunk into a deep sleep. Suddenly I opened my eyes and couldn't move besides from blinking, I lay on my side paralyzed and felt that someone kneeling on my bed behind my back, a pressure had been created in the mattress. Someone's elbow pressed into my right arm and I felt pain.

I saw that it was a male figure with a bull's head with thick glowing gold horns, which emerged from the upper part of his forehead. The pain in my right arm gradually intensified. I decided to speak with him voicelessly and politely asked him to leave and not bother me. I heard a devious laughter from his throat. I summoned angels and entities to come and help me.

He applied force on my right arm, approached my right ear and whispered:

*"Who do you think you are to dare write about me in your book? You mustn't write what you've intended to or slander my name. You are unaware of the fact that I have a respectable position in the universe **in order to allow a free choice** to all. You shall never publish the name of the book you've read and if you will do so - then I will visit you again... And while I'm here let's testify your forces."*

He applied increased force on my right arm and that was so painful. Suddenly I felt a *"ball of light and fire"* stirring in my belly and it reached my chest, entered my right arm which rose up and pushed him away.

The Prince of Darkness / Devil disappeared in an instant.

I decided to share that encounter in order to make it clear:

The devil does exist and has a place in the universe. I realized that good and evil do not exist. Maybe what's good for one person - is bad for the other. Everything is relative.

Everything exists around you in pairs:

Male and female; day and night;

darkness and light;

devil and angels; heaven and hell.

You even have been given the ability to lie

Because always telling the truth will

avoid you to choose. All is done in order to balance

and allow you a free choice.

My mother's death

Six months before my mother's death, while she was still clear-minded, I had a dream in which my mother appeared alone in a room and told me:
"Hash.... don't tell anyone that I'm here. Only you can see me. They are asking me in heaven to decide whether to stay here or to leave. What do you suggest I decide? I replied: *"Mother, I have no right to decide for you, that is a decision **only you** can make."* She replied back: *"O.K, I'll think what I should do",* after that, I saw the number <u>five</u>.

I didn't tell anyone about the dream and kept it to myself, not to pressure or intimidate others.

Friday at four o'clock in the afternoon, I received a message in my head: *"You must rash to the hospital".* So I got in my car and began driving toward the hospital. I felt that my mother was sitting in the passenger seat beside me, she said:

"I came to say goodbye. I chose to leave now, on a Friday afternoon when there is little traffic on the roads because I know how much you hate traffic jams." I replied:

"Mother, wait for me! I want to say goodbye before you go. I will be arriving at the hospital shortly."

She also gave me some messages to give to other. I entered the hospital and ran to her room, few relatives told me:

*"Your mother passed away **while you were driving"**.*

As my mother was lying on the bed, I saw a vision which she was standing, smiling, healthy, happy and suffered no pain while she was entering *'The tunnel of light'*. Then I found myself passing personal messages from her to a few relatives and even to the medical staff, all were shocked from the precision.

Friday at **five** o'clock in the evening, my mother passed away as in my dream! **Remember that we are all made of souls; therefore we cannot die and life keeps on moving:**

*The soul is infinite. Each soul enters a host body - at the time of birth and exits it - at the time of death, then the soul transfer back to a spirit. Each event that occurred in your lives **was meant to be - because you chose it!** All to achieve personal empowerment, mature, to complete cycles and make a correction with your karma.*

You have received the most precious thing which no one else can give you and that is **life - the only sacred thing.**

You have received from your parents

the most precious thing on earth,

which no one else can give you:

 life - the only sacred thing.

You cannot die.

You are an infinite soul that testifies on herself

by learning through being in

a temporary material body,

to attest to the nature of the soul's spirit

and of The Creation / God's spirit.

෴

Fear results from - the lack of knowledge.

Knowledge is power - which chases fear.

If you know - then there is nothing to fear.

In every aspect of life,

*the moment you ask '**why**' and*

do not receive a logical answer,

it is the time to stop and rethink the matter.

The soul is infinite.

It enters a host body at the time of birth

and exits it at the time of death.

The soul returns 'home' to God as a spirit.

Each event that occurred in your lives

was meant to occur - because you chose it!

You chose to experience those events in order

to achieve personal empowerment and mature

and to complete cycles and finally,

make correction with your own karma.

If you will rid yourself of fear

and constantly practice,

you will improve your

abilities to receive messages

and knowledge as well

into your intuition sense.

Pay attention to every detail

of your day-to-day lives.

'The creation' is trying to provide

you with messages such inside:

Book, song or anything else you read, hear or see.

Once there was a child girl that was a bit odd,
a little shy but with a heart of gold.
She wanted to help those around her
so they would see, how much kindness God gave her.
She asked to feel like she belonged somewhere,
to experience care and love with one another.

She had no books or toys on her shelf,
so she imagined another life and created lots of games
from cardboard and colored pencils for herself.

When she had no doll to hold,
she made one from a sock that was old.
She played hide and seek by herself and didn't think it was odd
to always have conversations with God.

She spent her childhood in the backyard of an old house,
many years ago in a distressed neighborhood.

She was blessed with the ability to receive and correspond
with entities that gave her messages
from the hidden worlds beyond
which in time were revealed to be true
And so she helped other people and her reputation grew.

Channeling gave her happiness, satisfaction ,and friends.
She didn't have much fortune - but a heart of gold
which was provided to her - by Almighty **God.** "

❧ Chapter 1 ❧

Who are we and where do we come from?

How did humanity first settle planet Earth?

Is man really a descendant of the gorilla or not?

How does all connect with the period of the Bible and th dinosaurs?

Who wrote the books of the Bible? What are the Ten Commandments? Were there more or less than ten?

As a great believer in *The Creation* (*God*), I respect religion but I'm not religious thanks to the freedom of choice.

I do not belong to any organization, political party, movement or sect. I have no desire or motivation to becom a guru or to glorify one person or another, certainly not myself.

All religions contradict the human being's right to freedom of choice. The moment a person is given a list of doing and don't, he is prevented for him the option to decide.

A few insights:

1. **If there was only one single truth** then it would be pretty boring to focus on it all the time rather than invent new ideas each and every moment.

2. **Every book is written from the viewpoint and education of its author** according to his period time. The smart thing is to consider a variety of opinions in order to achieve an open-minded way of thinking.

3. As everything else in life, in order to understand you should **always listen to both sides,** that is why we have both ears. Similar to a judge who listens to both parties and reaches a decision.

4. The possibilities are there, to allow us a choice! that is the reason why there are numerous religions, faiths, languages, educational methods, sexual and nutritional preferences, organizations, businesses and so on.

5. It is very important that the inhabitants of planet Earth adopt a single global language: The English language, preferably the British version, which is characterized by tolerance and respect for nature and acceptance of the other. In addition *'The creation'* recommends to all humanity not to hunt and kill animals for eating or as a hobby.

Using English as a single language will help to communicate and will unify all of Earth's inhabitants.

Today the English language is the universal language. It time to let go of stubbornness and ego about whether "yours or mine language is ancient or better'.

Although every nation has the right to learn and preserve its own ancient language.

Humanity must continually make progress, without being stuck in the past history.

It is unnecessary to preserve the history

since humanity never learned the

lessons of the past and still repeats the

same mistakes over and over again.

Did the wars of the past teach

us to strive for peace?

Or have we only learned to

improve the technologies of the

weapons and the methods

of spying and destruction?

It is surprising that most of the religion book display continuity, the unified chronological sequence of events, spanning thousands of years and "miraculously" gathered into a single book. How is this possible?

Religious and history books, like all books, are written from the personal viewpoint of their authors; **they only represent their "truth".** As you know, there are two sides to every coin, which is way, you always must hear the other side, opinion to understand the complete truth.

Remember: The other side will always have his own 'truth', which is different from yours but still it's the same story with two sides of view.

Many scientific, religious and historical books discuss in great detail about the prehistoric man, the prehistoric era, and history in general. Many authors have written about each individual subject, but few have connected all the dots as this book does!

❧ God, The Creators and The Created ❧

God / The Creation

The meaning of this word is :
God or the 'creation's entities'
that constantly replicate themselves and
recreate the universe in every moment.

God created **'The creators'**
so they could create **'The created'**.
In the entire Universe one human race
is creating other human races.

God / The Creation is an infinite cosmic energy, full of light and love. It creates endlessly world's, stars, souls while it duplicates itself nonstop.

The Creators

- *'The creators'* are responsible for creating various humanity and other life forms on Earth.

  The creators cannot create universes, stars, darkness, light, souls, etc.
  only *God / The Creation* can.

- Additional names of *'The creators'* are:
  certain kind of Extra-terrestrial / Aliens from other planets which exist in various life forms in *the* infinite Universe.

  'The creators' must adhere to the universe law: freedom of choice for all, therefore they must allow as to have freedom of choice (rule No. 1).
  But they supervise everything that is done on their planet Earth and try not to interfere*.

  *Only when things are getting out of control (see chapter 12) than *'The creators'* offer assistance in order to prevent mankind from annihilating itself.

Planet Earth is used as a

experimental laboratory

of 'The creators'.

With the aid of advanced

technologies from other planets.

'The creators' have created

'The created': the mankind.

In a process of Hybridized animal (a male gorilla)

with a bright entity (an alien female).

The Created

The creators created **all Earth mankind = those are *The Created* by hybridized between a male gorilla and a femal alien** possessing free choice.

The mission of all humanity and all life form around the universe is: to create! As this book: Divine creation!

God / The Creation

A cosmic energy, which created the universe and doubles itself to infinity.

The Creators

Are certain kind of Extra-terrestrial / Aliens, which created all Earth mankind.

The Created

Are all Earth mankind, who are also designed to create an advanced human being, which will create another advanced human being on other planets and so on in infinite creation.

In the beginning, God created

The entire Universe exists in the darkness. *God / The Creation* was a bit 'bored' in the vast darkness, then decided to create life forms and worlds to introduce some l.i.g.h.t into the darkened, to make Universe more dynamic and interesting.

"And God saw the light, that it was good":

These words testify to the fact that **God / The Creation** created the Universe through a process of trial and error and this is how it has always been: **God / The Creation** creates, operates, changes, upgrades and corrects.

1 "In the beginning, God created the heaven and the earth

2 And the earth was without form and void, and darkness was upon the face of the deep. And the Spirit of God moved upon the face of the waters.

3 And God said, Let there be light: and there was light.

4 And God saw the light, that it was good: and God divided the light from the darkness.

5 *And God called the light Day, and the darkness he called Night. And the evening and the morning were the first days.*

16 *And God made two great lights; the greater light to rule the day, and the lesser light to rule the night: he made the stars also.*

17 *And God set them in the firmament of the heaven to give light upon the earth,*

18 *And to rule over the day and over the night, and to divide the light from the darkness: and God saw that it was good".*

Verse Number 1:

1 *"God created the heaven"*

The infinite space, where one cannot naturally walks in the physical dimension, but in the spiritual dimension as a soul.

"And the earth"

***God / The Creation* created the planets / Earth** within infinite space; the Earth is where one can naturally walk in the physical dimension.

"And the earth was without form and void"

In the Big Bang, **God / The Creation** chose to create souls and planets. In order to do so, **it first created chaos, then selected one planet and one soul, shattered them** and from their seeds dust additional souls and planets were created.

"God made the stars also"

Each galaxy contains a number of **planets that emit light in the great darkness**: the Moon (which illuminates during the night) and the Sun (which illuminates during the day).

In each galaxy, life can exist on only one planet!

Therefore, of the nine planets in the Solar System, **life can exist only on planet Earth:**

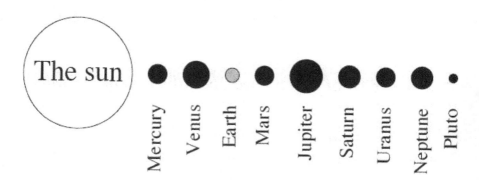

Verse Number 2

2 *"And the earth was without form and void, and darkness was upon the face of the deep. And the Spirit of God moved upon the face of the waters."*

"And the earth was without form and void"

Planet Earth was created in the Big Bang from **chaos without form.**

"And darkness was upon the face of the deep"

The Universe is **a bottomless void without boundaries** which also exists in the darkness that surrounds the Earth.

"And the Spirit of God moved upon the face of the waters"

God / The Creation consists of souls that **received life through the water and breathed life into a living body.** Where there is water - there is life.

Verse Number 3

3 "And God said, Let there be light: and there was ligh

God / The Creation 'said' let there be light and light was created.

- Everything that you say or think it's an energy, that **returns to you.**

- **Everything exists in the present,** in layers upon layers, s there is no past-present-future in the structure of time.

- There are no concepts of time in the Universe, only lightyear concepts.

- **Humanity invented the time,** in order to define the space of his own movements.

Verse Number 4

4 "And God saw the light, that it was good"

God / The Creation **created the light** using the trial and error method and saw that it was good and beneficial.

Other than tiny dots of light that are emitted from stars, **the entire Universe exists in darkness.**

This testifies to the fact that Darkness was created first and then light. Darkness is a natural state of the Universe.

Darkness existed long before the light was created.

Everything exists within the darkness and through the light.

Light helps to reveal what already exists in the darkness.

You were created from darkness and to darkness you shall return.

The darkness is the only thing that is unchanging and perpetual which connects all parts of the Universe.

Accept the darkness as a background color upon which you can shine your internal light.

Darkness should not be feared. People give it mistaken connotations of evil and the unknown. Light is temporary, local and emitted from stars. **Darkness is the natural state.**

All creation of life occurs in the dark, such as:

The birth and death of all mankind and even stars, the fertilization of the woman, creation of the fetus with all the various stages of pregnancy.

Verse Number 5

5 "And God called the light Day, and the darkness he called Night. And the evening and the morning were the first days".

God / The Creation allowed both light and darkness to exist at their proper times. The light during the day and the darkness during the night. It allows order and rests for mankind, that the night and the morning together will make up a single day.

Verses 16 – 18

16 "And God made two great lights; the greater light to rule the day, and the lesser light to rule the night: he made the stars also".

17 And God set them in the firmament of the heaven to give light upon the earth,

18 And to rule over the day and over the night, and to divide the light from the darkness: and God saw that it was good".

"And God saw that it was good".

This is the continuation of the **trial and error experiment,** an experiment that succeeded -"God saw that it turned out well".

God / The Creation decided to **illuminate the darkness of the Universe** with some local celestial flashlights (just like street lights illuminate large areas).

In the realm of the lesser light- the Moon- illuminates during the short night and in the realm of the greater light- the Sun- illuminates during the long day.

The daytime is much longer than the nighttime in order to allow mankind **to discover throughout the day, that which exists in darkness.**

☙ The settlement on planet Earth ☙

It all began with a single bang - the Big Bang.

In order to create - chaos must first be produced.

Like when you renovate a house, at first there is a lot of mess and disorder. Once things are put into order, repaired or replaced, then a new order is achieved.

A brief explanation of The Creation process:

In the Big Band, a single soul and a single planet were collided, exploded and shattered all over the Universe and cloned itself to a limited number of souls and planets.

When the guiding logic is that this process, of star replication, is repeated throughout the universe, colliding planets and their stardust are nonstop producing new planets yet the number of souls in the universe remains the same.

In order for a soul to enter a human body at birth, another must leave another body at the time of death.

First, *God / The Creation* created water: the foundation for the existence of life on Earth. It was done by sending enormous meteors of ice to Earth. That's how oceans and seas were created.

Second, volcanoes were created as nature developed and life forms took shape on planet Earth. Then *'The creators'* (Aliens) arrived and created a new human breed on Earth.

Life on Earth begun billions of years ago with
*a **'leasing' agreement** between*
***God / The Creation** and 'The creators'*
to create a new human breed
by Hybridization between
a male Gorilla and a female Alien on Earth.

Boundaries

Human beings find it difficult to **accept the fact they live in a black hole within a boundless universe.**

This difficulty results from the 'fear of the unknown' that causes human beings to fight and conquer, to establish laws and create rules in order to produce their own 'order':

- Boundaries in time and date.
- Boundaries at sea and in the air
- Boundaries between countries, territories, etc.

The Universe is boundless and so are the earth and the sea
Open a window and you will see that nature does not exist
straight lines and all lines are crooked and connect togeth
In this period, life on Earth is restrictive and doesn't allow
for personal freedom.

Here are a few explanations:

- Luckily enough, the air on Earth is boundless and limitless. It is everywhere and crosses into space.
- The continents and oceans on the surface of planet Earth were created without any boundaries and limitations and were given to all mankind equally regardless of religion, race, gender or nationality.
- The moment a Man's movement on Earth is limited; his freedom of choice (rule 1) is denied. This negative energy returns in a cyclical movement (rule 2) and creates wars among human beings.

Because of **the lack of freedom**, as a result of deep awarenes and excessive use of 'force of law' beyond the boundaries of reason, this is a necessary chaos for citizens to demonstrate rebel and fight against governments and regimes.

Rule 2- 'All returns', this 'force action' from the governmen return back to her, which invests financial resources in suppressing their citizens in order to maintaining their 'boundaries and rules' they themselves invented. It is surreal.

Human beings, out of ego and existential fear, have conquered lands by force, declared them to be their own, separated themselves from other with borders on sea and land, and have given themselves their own identifying marks, such as flag, nationality, religion, language, and culture. Humanity cannot see the complete picture:

Human beings may be different from one another in their appearance, language and opinions, but they all possess a soul, this is common to all of mankind. All souls belong to a single mother soul. In the Big-Bang, a single soul and a single planet shattered.

Everyone was created naked and possessing freedom of choice and has the right to live, work, study, learn, travel, eat, dress and be born or buried wherever they choose in any country regardless of borders and government permission. In the future, from the year 2106, there will be a global government without boundaries. See in my second book: The Future/2018, Lucy)

Human beings will never own materials. The only thing humanity owns: is not their fortune or soul - **but only their freedom of choice.**

❧ The Dinosaurs ❧

Once the Earth was endowed only with the elements of nature, *The creators* decided to populate the planet with animals on the sea and on land. They conducted many experiments on their planet and created many types of animals, male and female for breeding purposes and brough them to planet Earth in **Noah's Ark**, which was their spacecraft.

- Over billions of years, *The creators* had **performed many experiments** on their animals on Earth. Over the time, th growth of the animals went out of control and they reached enormous dimensions. That was the age of the dinosaurs, then The creators decided to end that era and to start anew. *The creators* collected to a spacecraft (Noah's ark) many animal species, male and female for future breeding.

- **In order to create again, first, there must be chaos.** This was produced by **The Flood**, a deluge of enormous **meteor made of ice** and originating from the rings that surround the Earth. Even after the meteors were burnt in the Earth's atmosphere, they remained large enough to destroy life on Earth but planet Earth.

- Then Earth underwent cataclysmic change, which started the **Ice Age**. Eventually, the Earth thawed and returned to a state that would allow the existence of life again.

- Once the Earth could be inhabited again *The creators* **returned to Earth** in a spacecraft /Noah's Ark with many animal species (male and female) which were collected before The Flood and **upgraded since then.**

- Based on past experience, *The creators* decided to populate the Earth not only with animals but also with human beings who they created in a **crossbreeding process between animal (male Gorilla) and Alien (female).**

'God / The Creation created man in his own image

All souls were created from a divine spark of God's spirit and will exist forever.

All living forms/ 'The Created' on Earth were created by 'The creators' / Aliens which leave them on Earth to merge and mingle between themselves in order to allow endless creation.

❧ The creation of Mankind ❧

The creators /Aliens created *The Created* by:
three species of human beings on Earth by crossbreeding a male Gorilla with a female Alien.

- The Japanese were created first. They are the most ancient nation. Japan is the country that invented and refined global technology from the 1970s' to 1980s':

  Sony, TOSHIBA, TEAC, JVC, AKAI, SHARP, Fujitsu, Panasonic, Pioneer, Nikon, YAMAHA, CASIO etc.

- Creation of man began billions of years ago in Japan, they are the most similar to their Creators / the aliens/ From there, humanity spread globally through Asia.

Throughout the Universe, there are countless human species, each with its own form, look and features. While we are known by the name 'human beings' they are known by various other names. Each creator has a destiny of creating creates and so are the humanity on Earth.

❧ The origin of the Human Race ❧

The creators are Aliens from distant planets. They created the three races of human beings on Earth. They first created the Japanese as their appearance :

- High about five feet tall.
- Skinny bodies with long hands that reach their knees. A small mouth and large and slanted eyes with dark pupils without eyelashes or body hair
- Bumps on their faces that serve as nostrils but no external nose bone.

The Aliens communicate mainly through telepathy and by writing symbols with emotionless robotic thinking.

The Japanese also have a lot of rituals and code of conduct of their own, working around the clock, acting like robots with inhuman standards and show little emotion and their written language made of symbols.

Similarities:

A lower percentage of DNA from the aliens /extraterrestrials:

Short, straight black hair; small and flattened nose.

A higher percentage of DNA from the aliens /extraterrestrials:

Slanted eyes, skinny and short. Their body is hairless, similar language and writing; they have a robotic and often emotionless way of thinking.

Over the time, two additional human races were created by *'The creators'* according to the different climatic conditions on continents of the Earth.

By mating with each other, these three basic human species created a large variety of human types appearances, as they exist today.

Over the years, the climate and area of habitation influence the skin tone, hair ,and eyes of all three races and depending on the different levels of vitamin D that result from exposure to sunlight

The creators created three human races separated from ea
other:

The Asian Human Race - has a higher percentage of female
Alien DNA and a lower percentage of male Gorilla DNA.
This is how human beings were created, which are **similar**
their appearance to Aliens.

male Gorilla	female Alien

❧

The Dark-Skinned Race - has a higher percentage of male
Gorilla DNA and a lower percentage of female Alien DNA. Th
is how human beings were created, which are **similar in the**
appearance to Gorillas.

male Gorilla	female Alien

❧

The Light-Skinned Race - has a higher percentage of female
Alien DNA and a lower percentage of male Gorilla DNA. This
how human beings were created, which are **similar in their**
appearance to the average between the Gorilla and Alien.

male Gorilla	female Alien

Created first : ian man	Created second: **Dark-skinned** man	Created third: **Light-skinned** man
NA Crossbreeding tween orilla and **high percentage of** **male Alien.**	DNA Crossbreeding between female alien DNA and **A high percentage of** **Gorilla.**	DNA Crossbreeding between a Gorilla and **The average** **percentage** **between them.**
milarities: anted eyes, skinny nd short, straight air, sparse body hair. Vritten and oral anguage similar to ne alien one omposed of symbols nd shapes. obotic thinking, ften emotionless.	Similarities: Skin tone, hair and eyes: dark. Flattened nose, muscular, possesses a high level of physical power and testosterone. Thick curly hair.	Similarities: Skin tone, short height, eye color: light. Hair types: Straight, wavy light and curly.
reas of habitat: Moderate climate. sia.	Areas of habitat: Warm climate. **Africa.**	Areas of habitat: Cold climate. **Europe.**

❧ The origin of Man and Woman ❧

man	woman
The origin of **man** is from **the Gorilla.**	The origin of **woman** is from **the Alien**
Similarities to Gorilla	**Similarities to Alien**
-Large body mass, large and high.	-Narrow, small, low body mass.
-Muscular upper body part and legs.	-Thin physique, narrow waist and refined face.
-possesses a high level of physical power and testosterone.	-Lower physical power and high level of spiritual and telepathic strength.
-Hunters who can perform one activity each time.	-As gatherer can perform multiple tasks at the same time as a computer performance.
-Aggressive, warriors, with egos and an inclination to rule as the head of the tribe.	-Delicate, well-groomed, caring, maternal, less ego, and more peace-loving.
-Less sentimental, and more logical mind.	-More sentimental for the other's needs.
-Occupations that require physical strength and logical thinking.	-Occupations that require integrated action, responsibility, help, tolerance and to educate.

The differences between man and woman

- **Woman** originates from **the alien /extraterrestrial**. She is able to perform multiple tasks like a computer. Such abilities prepared her to become a gatherer who is able to perform several simultaneous tasks.

- **Man** originates from **the gorilla**. He is a hunter who can perform mostly a single task each time. Men are busy with survival as animals; they possess ego and pride as the gorillas are 'the leaders of the pack' and other males in the animal kingdom.

- Statistically, **women have longer life spans** than men.

- In most cases, **women are more spiritual** than men. They possess intuition and a greater openness to receive messages and communications from the Universe. Therefore, women are usually involved in the spiritual world.

- **Migraines** most often affect women. Migraines are a spiritual factor which influencing the physical body when channeling ability is not expressed in practice

  Migraines = It is an energy that starts from the crown chakra (located at the top of the head) and descends to the third eye chakra (located in the forehead between the eyes) and controls the temples.

This is the process of receiving messages and communication with the Universe. If this information is not channeled outside ,therefore the energy creates a physical pressure on the forehead and temples area.

- **Men** were intended to perform projects that require **great physical strength**. Similar to gorillas, men are strong, sturdy, muscular and have a high level of testosterone which leads to hair growth all over their bodies including a beard and bristles.

Like gorillas, most men enjoy living in small packs and rule their kingdom like 'the king of the gorillas'.

This is why humanity began to organize in smaller tribes, villages and small family units.

Like the gorillas, the behavior of most men is based on ego and existential fear. As a result, they act violently and aggressively and they tend not to act out of emotion which they consider unmanly.

- **Men with feminine**, gay tendencies, came to Earth to balance and restrain destructive male power in the world/ Which is usually connected directly to their *karma* with whom they came to the world, in order to correct wrongs and destruction they had committed in their previous incarnations.

- **Women with a male bias**, lesbians, came to Earth to empower the status of women and end their karma of enslavement and repression from which they suffered from their previous incarnations.

- **Women are generally more refined** than men. As opposed to men, women are able to live in bigger tribes or large groups based on their desire for personal freedom. Women can share one husband with other women (just like the kings and rulers of the past who had several wives).

- **Man finds it difficult to share a woman** with other men because of his totalitarian outlook. A woman can share herself with several men without any physical or moral problem.

- **Women are aliens,** therefore are **multi-sexual**. It is common to see women of every age holding each other hands or kissing. Women are much more open-minded, both sexually and mentally and their emotional side is dominant, women can share their love with others, both males ,and females, without any difficulty.

- **Most men are heterosexual** gorillas who tend to recoil from touching other men. Most of them are jealous and demand that their women remain with them forever throughout their lives, while women seek out new loves and thrills in their lives. That is how the tension between the sexes began.

- **Unfaithfulness** arises from the need of a person's soul to experience love outside of a relationship, which a person doesn't want to undermine for various reasons of convenience. Unfaithfulness is not a "despicable crime".

The human soul is what pushes a person to be unfaithful. It's simply the basic need of a human being to reach for love as love is the fuel of the soul because without love humanity will become ill.

Remember the first rule: The only thing that you own is your freedom of choice and it should not be touched. It the right of any person to experience love without been forced to act in a way that contradicts the will of his soul

- **The women bring balance** that counteracts the men's destructive powers. Men mostly act out of emotionless common sense, ego ,and existential fear. If not for women men would bring about the destruction and annihilation of humanity on Earth. The pages of history are filled with stories of wars and conflicts that were planned and executed by men.

- **The role of women on Earth is to balance the wild and animalistic power of men**: whose origin is from the ape which is strong, dominating and the 'leader of the pack'. Therefore, the vast majority of world leaders are men.

- It is true that in order to become pregnant a female needs male sperm (a process that will change in the future) yet the entire process of insemination and pregnancy takes place only within the female's body. The source of the female is *'The creators'*, which can create life, therefore **females are the cosmic alien factory.**

⮂ Everything exists forever⮂

Each tree that is uprooted and every fruit that is plucked - will grow again.

A forest destroyed by fire or a polluted ocean – will recover. Everything is perpetually renewed!

If we look at a piece of material, such as: wood, cloth, glass, plastic or metal, under a microscope we will discover that the atoms are constantly moving because everything exists forever! In each and every state of matter and form!

Nothing can go extinct or be killed. Even in death, the soul leaves the body which is perishable and returns to inhabit a different body, if it so chooses.

Nature is everything whatever lives and breathes inside you and everything around you.

Nature is the Earth: everything that grows, the air, human beings and animals (from the germs – and up to mankind).

Everything breathes, multiplies, expands and contracts.

Nature is everyone's element of life.

Without nature - there is no life!

You cannot silence, destroy or stop anything in nature.

Everything lives and exists forever.

Nature, air and light

Air and light are full of an energy, called 'Prahna' which means a *force of life, breath, soul or cosmic power.* It is the **vibration that exists** in everything. 'Prahna' connects the organs of the physical body by the circulatory systems which lead to the heart.

'Prahna' connects the soul to the spiritual body through chakras and auras. Auras and Chakras are connected by do and lead to the soul. While looking at air or water in daylight, **one can see the 'Prahna' as rounded shapes, transparent spheres** (often with a center dot) in various colors which can often be captured with a camera.

Music and scents also have colors and shapes of their own which can be perceived through the ten senses.

The physical body = the male aspect.

The soul = the female aspect.

Air, light, earth, water ,and music are all part of the creation's vibrations. Such vibrations influence the emotional and energetic body of all souls.

Preserving planet Earth

Essentially, you are a soul that inhabits for a short time a living body on the face of the Earth. As a soul, you can change identities and bodies in each incarnation.

The physical body has no life without your presence as a soul.

Human beings have an egotistical way of thinking as if everything is permitted since 'we own it all', this type of egotistical viewpoint could bring to the destruction of nature and the environment. For example in these days:

Land and water resources are polluted, consumed and destroyed.

: Animals are slaughtered excessively on land and in the sea

"Whales and dolphins must not be killed. These are ancient animals that conceal within them the 'secret of the Creation'. These are not the ones in danger of extinction - **_human beings are!_** *"*

"You are all guests for a short stay on the face of the Earth. You are all souls who have been lent to you, souls that in each incarnation, choose a host body and breathe life into it, you don't possess anything in the Universe other than your own freedom of choice".

The elderly and the ancient

"Stand up in the presence of the aged and show respect for the elderly and what is ancient".

This verse, calls on us not only to revere the elderly but also to revere nature which is ancient and which existed before human beings were created.

All of mankind's actions come back to him (Rule No. 2) so, therefore:

The moment humanity destroys the resources of nature, future generations will no longer possess the basis for life and they will gradually become extinct.

The moment mankind goes too far, *'The creators'* will create a chaos by sending meteors to Earth, in order to destroy mankind but not the foundations of planet Earth and the sources of life.

Tip for life

- Work, study, eat and drink moderately.

- Learn to touch and demonstrate love, show tolerance and care for one another. **The lower level of love reveals itself through sexuality and the higher level through compassion.**

- Expand your horizons, travel and enjoy nature.

- Get to know your neighbors all across the globe, with respect and tolerance.

The memories and insights

you gather during your lifetime

are the only things you will take with you

to your next incarnation.

At the moment of death, when you reach 'the heavens' you will be asked the following by *'The creation'*:

"What have you done to benefit yourselves and the environment? What mission have you completed?"

In other words, you will be asked the following:

Have **you** experienced love, what have **you** learned, what kind of education and insights have **you** achieved for yourself, what have **you** seen, how have **you** advanced humanity and yourself as souls and how have **you** helped the people and the environment with your knowledge?

You would not be asked: *"How many children you had or how much money you earned. These are not the missions of life".*

❧ Chapter 2 ❦

God, religion
and other Insights

❧ Who is God / The Creation? ❧

Who is God? What does he look like?

What language does he speak?

Why doesn't he reveal himself to us?

There are no religions in the Universe, but only faith.

- It is an infinite cosmic energy full of light, love which duplicates itself constantly and exists everywhere and in everything. It creates worlds, stars, and souls and makes the Universe go around perpetually and It is the source c religions, sects, nations and languages. It gave human beings freedom of choice so they could choose. God speaks all languages and religions.

- It is wrong to ascribe to it human emotions, such as anger, hatred or "the wrath of God". These are all humar conceptions.

- It is not 'an old man' dressed in white and sitting up in th heavens. It is asexual gender-free and doesn't have a physical body. It often manifests 'itself' in a physical body on Earth.

- It is everywhere in spirit and in the matter, which renews themselves in a cyclical and endless way.

- **Nothing is yours except your freedom of choice.** All were given to you by its grace, every book, article, invention, knowledge or idea is originates from *God / The Creation!*

You were created by 'The creator' in order

to testifies to the nature of you and God / The Creation!

How would you know who you are without looking in a mirror of your soul?

Each and every one of your actions testify to the nature of God / The Creation.

How can God / The Creation know whether it is good, merciful, loving, generous, helpful, hateful, cruel or miserly?

❧ Insights about religion ❧

God / The Creation did not create religion - human beings did. There are no religions in the Universe - but only FAITH.

Religion was created by human beings:

1. To prevent from the primitive nature of human beings from ruining themselves and their environment.

2. Human beings find it difficult to live without boundaries (although the Universe has no boundaries) plus adding

the 'The freedom of choice' to people make it much more difficult to control them.

3. Ever since, human beings have sought a "responsible adult" to take care of them and take them under his wing, like a child attached to his parents. Human beings seek supervision out of fear of themselves and their own actions.

4. Human beings always will search for their creator and found many ways to channel with **God / The Creation** and parts of this communication are documented in the ancient books (the Bible).

5. The initial goal of inventing religion was to connect the material (the human body) and the spiritual (the soul) with **God / The Creation**, to whom the souls of all belong.

6. However, over time religion became more powerful and a way to solve or escape one's troubles. As religion grew stronger the use of force and intimidation increased often accompanied by coercion and threats, brainwashing of false promises and lies. History testifies to this up to this days.

7. **In a place where there are knowledge and high education, religious coercion loses its power.**

- **God / The Creation** is made up of a cosmic energetic spirit of love which surrounds all that is taking place in the Universe as a powerful endless a tornado that renews and duplicates itself at every given moment.

Only one thing is sacred - life (soul), start getting used to it: There are no sacred places - but only ancient places. There are no sacred books - but only ancient books.

- *God / The Creation* does not reveal his real image to human beings because its energy mass is so vast that it could cause spiritual damage to all material creatures.

- *God / The Creation* did not create religion or temples; they were created by human beings. It only wants you to acknowledge his existence and will never ask you to worship him because it knows his glory. In the same way, you don't worship your parents who brought you into the world.

- *God / The Creation* never asked you for anything material or to make sacrifices, build prayer houses or worship with daily prayers, to turn your lives into blind worship. It also didn't ask for coffins or tombstones. Those originating from the rites and ceremonies from the past.

- *The creators* are alien species that created you in the same way that *other creators* created other breeds of humans on other planets in the Universe and so on.

- **God / The Creation helps those who help themselves.** A man must first show some effort in order to receive the help. Prayer has a wonderful power to create as all

imagination: **as the moment to imagine - you create!
Every thought, saying and deed creates reality as an energy
coming back to you.** There is no problem to gather and
pray together as long as it is done out of free choice.

- Remember: being good will bring you goodness in return
and will testify about **God / The Creation** .

- **God / The Creation** will not decide or limit you and will
not interfere with your freedom of choice.
Religion denies mankind's freedom of choice.
Religion dictates holidays and laws for its believers
because they are committed to doing as they are told, in
that way it denies them their free choice. The more
extremist and forceful the religion is, the more it is
removed from free-will and **God / The Creation** .

- **Religion and the male ego are the reasons for segregation
and war between nations.** As proof, one only needs to lead
through the pages of history. **God / The Creation** is full
of love. There are no punishments nor "God's Chariots"
nor "God's wrath". God will never hate or punish you.

- After your death, **God / The Creation** will not punish
you but will give you the chance to judge yourself and to
explain your essence where you went wrong. **You are
been loved for eternity.**

- **Everything takes place sequentially and simultaneously.
There is no past or future only the present exists.** You are
creating a new present in every single moment, layers

upon layers. Every action cancels the previous one and creates a new one, that's *the creation's engine*.

- **The ancient writings (Bible) are in part a collection of stories.**
  Ancient writings and the various books of any Bible were written by various authors who documented over the course of many generations various events in their own words and according to their personal viewpoint. Some of the events did actually take place in reality, while others were invented through legends, folk tales, and stories.

- **The ten commandments is a fraud:** Everything is written in the requirements without permits, as 'you shall not do this or that' in order to control humans.
  God / The Creation will never dictate you but provides all with free choice.
  Did you ever stop to think for a moment what is allowed if everything is forbidden? Where's the 'you shall do and enjoy?' Where are the choice and the fun? Perhaps someone omitted those commandments on purpose.

  Try to picture yourself going on a trip and from the very beginning, the guide imposes various commands and prohibitions. You think to yourselves 'If that's the way the trip begins, I'm definitely not going to have fun'.

- **God / The Creation speaks in all languages.** It created all languages. There is no need to actually speak. Silence has its own language.

- *God / The Creation* **dwells within you**
  It is a spirit that dwells within your body and outside of it in everything. There is no point in seeking it out in material objects, in distant lands, in the mountains, temples, prayer houses, tombstones or in ancient places.

- **All souls belong to God / The Creation . The quantity of souls is limited.**
  In the Big Bang, a single soul exploded and spread across the infinite Universe. All souls belong to that single divine soul.

  All souls are infinite and the number of souls in the Universe is fixed, limited and must be balanced between the planets in the Universe. **Currently, there is a population explosion** as a result of the uncontrolled birth rate, **therefore man's actions produce imbalance and deprivation, by forcibly taking souls from other planets, that will cause to fertility on Earth.**
  In order for a soul to enter a body, another soul needs to exit a body, parallel pathway for birth and death.

- **Human beings find it difficult to understand the world with endless limits and boundaries.**
  This is all too difficult for them to understand, so they created boundaries, limits, laws, measurements, time, quantities, sizes, territories, borders and etc.

- **The soul of the newborn enters its body only at birth – at the time it takes its first breath. A situation in which two souls inhabit one living body is impossible.**

The fetus feeds and breathes through the umbilical cord attached to its mother.

Therefore, Abortion is not considered murder because the soul of the baby had not yet entered its body (Women can be with a clean conscience).

The soul of the fetus enters its body only when it is already outside the womb at the time of birth when it takes its first breath.

In order to reign in the primitive nature of humanity, men of power with a narrow and strict view of the world, chose to remove from the ancient writings any possibility to allow human beings a free choice.

This is how religions began to control human beings by claiming that this is "what God commanded".

Since when does God give commands?

Make demands? Give out punishments?

God / The Creation will never use force,

but only the spirit of love

"Neither by might nor by power,

but by my spirit, I am the LORD ".

The biblical story of Abraham and Sarah

These are the responsible for the ongoing Karma between Arabs and Jews

Abraham and his wife Sarah lived in ancient times. Even while they lived in Egypt. the beautiful Sarah caused Abraham many problems. Pharaoh fell in love with Sarah because of her beauty and when he found out that she was Abraham's wife, he banished them from Egypt to Canaan (Israel). There are no coincidences because everything that happens including exiles and holocausts is intended to serve a noble and good cause.

Sarah was barren, so she decided to bring Hagar, her handmaid, to be Abraham's second wife. Hagar and Abraham had a son named Ishmael.

After the birth of Ishmael, 90-year-old Sarah became 'miraculously' pregnant with the aid of the three messengers. She gave birth to Isaac. Sarah acted out of jealousy and convinced Abraham to banish Hagar and Ishmael into the desert with only a jug of water and bread.

The meaning of the names Sarah and Hagar:

The name 'Sarah' (in Hebrew 'Zh'ara') contains bad energy and means jealous trouble woman who has a narrow point of view. Most women named Sarah have a difficult life or destiny.

The name Hagar (in Hebrew 'Lehager') which means to immigrate, and the word 'Ger' means foreigner.

The meaning of the names Ishmael and Isaac:

The name Isaac (in Hebrew 'Itzhak'), which means will laugh, shout or cry for help.

The name 'Ishmael' which means in Hebrew: listen to God,

The Arabs, who are descendent of Ishmael, want the Jewish nation to listen and respect them but the Jewish Nation prefers to laughs or shouts at them.

- To this very day, the descendants of Ishmael are angry about this injustice from the time of Abraham. Abraham was a rich man yet he gave Hagar and Ismael nothing but a jug of water and bread. Ishmael and Hagar were forced to immigrate; they were sent into the desert in an unjust way and without any possessions.

- Ishmael presents the Arabs which haven't got the respect, justice, inheritance or birthright then and seek those rights from his half-brothers the Jews to this day. This is a Karma cycle that has gone on for thousands of years.

- ***God / The Creation*** acts between 'freedom of choice' (rule No.1) and 'All returns' (rule No. 2). Such an injustice creates Karma energy that returns to its sender, justice will be made through chaos.

Abraham and Sarah
are the ancient ancestors
of the **Jewish nation of Israel.**

Abraham and Hagar
are the ancient ancestors
of **the Arab nations.**

The Jewish nation is the driving engine for
the Arab nations to raise up and lift itself
as they are half-brothers.

ॐ

"Dear Arabs and Jews
You are brothers; learn to live side by side
and respect one another.
Arabs - don't be jealous of the Jews
but aspire to them

The Creation has reduced from both so that
you will complement each other.

That which was not given in the past will be given!
For the problem will not be solved by the sword,
but with words of justice, recognition and love".

Is it possible that a tiny country like Israel makes such global noise?

The Jews nation designation is to bring light and message to all other nations include the Arabs nation, in the same way, that Jesus was a Jew who brought a light and new message to the world.

The moment there will be peace in Israel - then there will be peace all over the globe.

The Jews nation should be admired, for taking this difficult role upon themselves: that is to bring enlightenment, divine messages, awareness, peace, and insights to the rest of humanity.

❧ Insights about Life ❧

1. It is impossible to die since you have an eternal soul.

Internalize this insight and your fear of death will disappear as your way of thinking will change, there won't be any reason to invest any more resources in armies, security, weapons, and wars. All resources will be available to serve the goals they were intended for:

Science and technology.

Education, medicine, and research.

Protecting human rights and preserving nature.

Finding alternative sources of energy other than oil, nuclear reactors and so on.

Humanity will benefit for generations from this realization. It will allow human beings to focus on their real destiny on Earth which is to safeguard Planet Earth and to advance technologically in order to create an advanced human race on planet Earth that will populate other planets.

2. You are not inventing anything – everything already exists. You've come to discover who you are by understanding - who you are not.

Nothing was ever brought from outside the confines of the Earth. All the information and knowledge, any new idea or invention already exists in *'The creation'* and all human being do is to reveal them by merely mixed, connected and 'recreated'.

3. Nothing is yours – you are guests here on Earth.

When you die, you will 'return home' to *'God/The creation'* as a soul, stripped of all the assets and wealth you have accumulated, stripped of the relationships you'v had. You will return as a soul laden with the insights and experiences of your last incarnation.

4. Planet Earth is 'The emotional planet'.

Planet Earth is navigated by the emotions of humankind. Being on planet Earth makes it difficult for souls to learn and survive.

The mass of the Earth causes everything to happen at a slow pace. This is in contrast to some other planets with lower gravity, where things happen at a quicker pace than on Earth.

Higher gravitational force - lengthens the time axis! This means that physical actions take a longer time to perform.

5. There are Ten Senses, rather than Five Senses.

Most human beings activate only five senses instead of the ten senses therefore, they activate only five senses they do not see the complete picture and therefore receive for themselves only bits and pieces of information. This can lead to depression, anger, wars, and a tendency toward self-destruction, suicidal tendencies and so forth.

6. In addition to the main lines, there are several parallel life lines.

Before you entered your body as a spirit, **you have chosen everything in advance,** such as: What family you will belong to and in what location you will be born (country/city). Your visual appearance and sexual preference. Your time of birth and death, the main lines are fixed (destiny) along with several parallel destiny lines that are unfixed.

You have selected all of the above, in order to allow yourselves a choice. This was out of a need to complete and correct that which you didn't have the chance to do i your previous incarnations.

7. Opposites were created in order to achieve balance and allow choice.

man and woman, day and night, the prince of darkness and the white angel, heaven and hell, truth and lies, matter and spirit, sky and earth and so on. If there were only one of these opposites existed you would be denied the freedom of choice.

You have been given the ability to tell lies. **If lying were denied to you then life on Earth would become very boring.** You wouldn't even enjoy a movie or the theatre which are based on scripts and performed by actors who memorize their lines.

8. There's no good and evil. Everything is relative.

What's good for one person - may not be good for anothe and vice versa therefore, there is no such thing as 'good or evil'. Everything is relative and always for your own benefit in the future to come.

9. The soul has no ego. The ego dwells in the physical body and is intended for survival. One of the lessons a human being must learn is to control and balance it.

10. The greatness of humankind is measured by

compassion which derives from tolerance, attentiveness, understanding and helping others.

Thanks to politics many wars are prevented. Remember declaration of war takes only a few hours but making peace takes many years.

11. Demonstrating love in public.

Here is a general misconception of humanity:

Why should negative energies be allowed? By watching physical and verbal violence, such as boxing, wrestling, martial arts, car racing and other demolition, gossip and rumors. On the other hand, demonstrating love publicly, fondling and making love in public is prohibited by law and can result in fines and even arrest.

Why is negative energy allowed while the positive energy of love is not? It's against any Common sense! Human beings have certainly created some strange rules for themselves.

Such prohibitions were originally invented by various religion members. Rules were dictated to humanity in the name of religion. Medical research indicates that a baby who is not touched and does not receive human love and warmth, will not survive. You are souls of light who must receive the warmth of touch and love in order to survive in a human body.

Human beings must learn to be closer to one another, touch and hug. Love, at its lowest level, manifests itself sexuality and at its highest level as compassion and caring.

12. Competitions.

The very term 'competition' - should not exist! Human beings who compete with one another activate physical and mental strengths, even cheat all in order to win. But who exactly are they beating?

Competitions were intended to separate humanity. Gain and loss cause the separation and the division of humanity. The right thing to do is to award certificates participation or appreciation in a competition.

In a beauty or singing competitions - beauty and a good voice are judged according to personal taste and the preferences in a particular time period. What is beautiful for one person – may be less for another.

In sports competitions - swimming, running, tennis, soccer, basketball and so forth. Is it really important to know which of the contestants has the better inborn physical ability?

In intellectual competitions - math, physics, chess, Sudoku, trivia and so forth. Is it really important to discover who has better mental capabilities?

The Nobel Prize is a positive example! It is awarded people who were given a contribution to humanity! *The* *common to all competitions is the wish to separate 'the winner' from 'the loser', in order to* **enhance and glorify the ego of humankind.**

13. Do not be ashamed of your bodies Do not be ashamed.

So why cover up? *The creators are* proud of you as their creations, so why are you ashamed of your bodies? Be proud! That body contains who you are.

You are beautiful - as you were created.

Sex is for both love and survival. The norms of religion and society restrict mankind's sexual freedom. Do not try to be like the others. There are a meaning and amazing fact, that there are no two human beings alike, who are not born from the same womb.

14. Throughout our lives, we search for our other half.

From the moment of your birth till the day you die, you are in a constant searching for finding your twin soul: through love, academic or spiritual education, employment, travel, etc.

As you grow and mature, your understanding and awareness of your spiritual component diminish in order for you to chase it.

❧ Chapter 3 ❧

The basic rules
of the universe

❧ Rule No.1 - Freedom of choice ❧

Freedom of choice is given to all.

You were born naked with a soul that loan to you for your journey inside a body of matter or human, with freedom of choice. **God and The creation will never deprive you of your freedom of choice, they will not touch it.**

Always remember to allow freedom of choice to others. Never force anything against another's will. If you do, you are eliminating their free-will (rule 1) and that will come back to haunt you, because 'All returns' (rule 2).

Every living thing has a soul then honor all living things around you. All of nature around you is alive; all have souls, including plants, animals, human beings and more. Even inanimate objects are alive, which means that under a microscope, their atoms move.

You have the right to choose for yourself and for the helpless.

In cases of the helpless people, who are not in a conscious state to make wise decisions, such as: children, the elderly, the sick, people with physical or mental disabilities and animals, you must offer them as many choices as possible accompanied by advice and possible solutions, in order to allow them free choice as if you were choosing for your own good. You should treat others as you would like others to treat you.

❧ Animal & nature rights ❧

I have asked the following question: *"Is it correct to slaughter animals for food?"*

The message was: *"Only if there is nothing left to eat because animals have souls".*

The creation passes the decision to the human being, to allow free choice. You may eat animals in moderation.

Nature must remain natural,
without interference and artificial activities.

The growth of crops and the breeding
of livestock should not be manipulate
by genetic engineering.

If you abuse animals and nature
then it will return to affect your life
because all you do - come back to you (rule no. 2).

Respect animals, for example:

- **Do not stuff chickens** inside tiny and crowded coops, with 24 hours a day lighting in order to enhance the production of eggs.

chickens lay their eggs in great suffering and the person who eats those eggs or chickens absorbs the harsh energy concealed in them. **Do not** destroy tender chicks.

- **Do not separate** calves from their mothers in order to produce veal (steak). **Do not** fatten geese. **Do not abuse,** beat, hunt or starve animals.

- **Do not imprison animals in zoos!** Their natural habitat is nature itself!

- **Do not pollute** drinking water, water sources, the lands, the air and the atmosphere. Do not cut down too many trees. Do not overfish the oceans, and the list goes on and on. **It must be in moderation.** All of the above serves as the basis for the future existence of humanity on Earth.

*"Only a **quarter of animals** can be slaughtered for food.*

*Only **a quarter of crops** can be harvested for food.*

*Only **a quarter of lands** can be used for*

housing and industrialization.

Any excessive activity will lead to a future shortage.

ॐ Rule No. 2 - All returns ॐ

Known as *Karma: "what goes around - comes around"*.

Think what's going on with you at this very moment, thanks to gravity you are firmly planted attached to the base of the Earth which is floating in space! Everything that surrounds you is alive. The Universe is a slow whirlpool that turns around the stars and planets. The force of this cyclical movement makes everything go around in circularity. There are no square or triangular planets

The entire universe consists of circular rings which expand and shrink, like human breathing.

Let's consider Einstein's formula and redefine it from the energetic aspect of the soul:

$$E = Mc^2$$

E = Energy = Consciousness or *God/ The Creation.*

M = Mass of matter = Every material has a mass.

C = Circular speed of light = The reincarnations of the soul are moving on the light axis, as 'time in the Universe' is measured by light years.

C2 = The number of reincarnations are multiplying in each incarnation.

I thought, I said, I acted = Consciousness mass. This is how you create energy.

Similar to the Universe,
when you think, speak or act - you create energy through
the vibration of two-sided reaction (rule No 1 and rule No
which go forward and then comes back to you.

All you do - will come back to you eventually, you are the creator of your life.

The Circles of Creation

The entire Universe is like a ping pong game: everything
that is sent - returns back to the sender (rule No 2).

Negative thoughts

If you curse or bewitch, then you create a vibration, an
energy which is sent, reaches its destination and then retur
to you eventually. This bad energy might affect your health
success, relationships, livelihood and more. That's why you
must avoid cursing or wishing evil to others.

This will happen even if someone else cursed or bewitched
for you, whether for payment or not because the request
came from you! And then both you and the person who did
the actual cursing - will eventually be affected because 'All
returns' (rule No. 2).

Positive thoughts

If you bless, support or send love then you create a vibration and an energy that reaches its destination and returns to you for the better because everything is cyclical and returns to you, the sender (rule No 2).

Do good deeds and perform acts of kindness; this has nothing to do with religion but creating your own life paths.

Here some cycles of creation through spoken sentences:

*"I have **no** job, I have **no** career, I have **no** love, I will never be employed..."*

In these words, you send a vibration, an echo to the universe. At the same moment, you establish a fact which returns to you, because *'I have no'* will bring *'I have no'*!

Therefore, instead of saying *'I have no'* or *'I don't have'* say: *"I'm about to find'*: *job, career, love, good prosperity"*.

There are two universal rules:

- **Freedom of choice (rule No.1)**
- **All returns (rule No.2)**
  These rules are interconnected in an endless cycle.
- *God / The Creation* **will never interfere** in your choices or decides for you.

Your every action is done out of free choice (rule 1)
which activates self-creation (thought, speech and action
and returns back to you (rule 2) and so on.

Rule 1:
Freedom of choice

Rule 2:
All returns

Before you entered your body as a soul :

- You have selected your current incarnation with various life lines and destiny without ego, in order to allow you to choose from several options.

- You can choose to be born with a disability, to undergo traumas, diseases that you will suffer throughout your life because the soul selects its destiny without ego before it enters the body, at the moment of birth.

- Of course, it is not easy to ceaselessly create positive thoughts in our day-to-day life. *The Creation* gives us tasks for our own good.

- In difficult situations, the tendency of a person is to withdraw within himself, to lose trust and to feel frustration. This all comes from ego, stubbornness, misunderstanding one's destiny and the correction that the soul needs to undergo. Everything that takes place is always for the best.

❧ The lines life ❧

1. Human beings possess free choice.

Even after a person is given a prediction of the future, he still possesses free choice, in order to fulfill his goals in the way he chooses. The decision to act and to fulfill these goals depends only on the person himself and this influences the future's prediction.

If a person chooses not to fulfill at a certain time, that which was predicted, then the Universe will bring him new challenges at a different time.

In other words, everything which is about to happen will be postponed or may fulfill earlier or even canceled, all is changing according to the person's choices.

A fixed main life line exists for every person.
In parallel, there are changing secondary life lines.

The secondary life line are changing in accordance with the person's choices. Therefore, predicting will never be 100%, because it is correct to the moment of the prediction, due that the life lines are always changing.

In the same way, there is no fixed condition and everything is moving around us as the Universe, Earth and other planets, even the time that human invent, is moving.

2. Those who deal with the spiritual world are human beings without any 'superpower'.

What makes such spiritual people, is their ability to channeled by using most of their ten senses. Predicting the future is not a simple task, it involves maneuvering betwee predicting to a person and allowing him the free choice.

God / The Creation prevented human beings from

*seeing and predicting everything, so they will not lose interest in life. The mystery is what keeps humanity activ and awake. The **ability to predict the future is limite** in order to preserve the freedom of choice, curiosity and the element of surprise and the curiosity .*

❧ Everything is foreseen, yet free-will exist❧

'Everything is foreseen'

You were born naked with a soul that was lent to you, mair and secondary life line and freedom of choice. *God / The Creation* will never decide for you or will take your soul without asking your permission.

The main life line is fixed and

never changes (*everything is foreseen*).

Before a soul enters a body, it chooses its life lines:

- Several options for locations, city and country in which it will be born.

- Several options of times, in which it will enter ,and leave the body (birth and death).

- Its gender and the nuclear family it will join.

The fixed main life lines and the secondary life lines are moving together and parallel to one another, crossing intersections, which were chosen in advance by the soul.

'Yet free will exists'

The secondary life lines are constantly changing,

As 'Gates' opening and closing (*free will exists*).

Gates: exist within the secondary life lines and **provide opportunities**, which you can exploit and implement in your life. Nothing will happen unless you act to achieve it.

Like changing stations those Gates offer you several options and times, to each action in your life. You must choose wisely and with correct timing; there are no coincidences!

Everything that happens is always for your best. Even if you have failed, it's a sign that you were supposed to pass through that mistake in order to correct.

Sometimes, people see themselves as 'victims of life'. They live their lives filled with self-pity out of ego, stubbornness and laziness. They do not try to change or to select a secondary life line, a different option or a different 'gate'.

They could use the aid of spiritual people who can provide them with tools, answers, and insights.

Such frustrated people, instead of bringing about change in their condition, choose to ignore and to repress their problems. They choose to live their past without building their future; they create dependency and burden on the environment, self-destruction or attempt to find redemption by subjugation to religions.

Their condition is not going to improve unless they choose to help themselves. God/ *The Creation* will help only those who begin to help themselves and will assist the one who let go the ego, listens, respects the other, asks to be changed.

The free choice of the soul allows you to select a new path anytime. You can switch, change, move forward or remove all according to your free will.

The future can be guessed and predicted, but remember that it's changing constantly depends on your choices, therefore the forecast is correct to the moment when the question was asked.

If everything was known in advance,

then you could not have free choice.

God / The Creation will not dictate

but rather **allows you to choose for yourself.**

Even if your choices are wrong,

you learn through your experience.

Please take the prediction which given to you

as an advice that sometimes comes true

and sometimes not, because it depends

on the free choice of all concerned

❧ Chapter 4 ❦

Death is impossible

Souls cannot die but change their identity.

Each living body serves as a vessel, through which the soul can manifest as matter and walk in the physical dimension on Earth. The destiny of all souls is to testify to the nature of *God / The Creation* through their actions.

The soul is the basis and the source of all spiritual and material living in the Universe. Souls exist in Earth, nature plants, water, animals, humans, aliens, entities, angels, etc.

At the time of death, at the end of the journey, the soul leaves the body, in which it was trapped and returns 'Home' to *God / The Creation* as a free spirit.

Your soul is an eternal spark of The Creation.

The soul, in its original state as a spirit,

breathes life into a temporary physical body

and returns to it spiritual state at the time of death.

The spirit has no beginning and no end.

Everything is eternal.

Death

Each death is a temporary transit station in the course of the infinite life.

You cannot and will not die, you only change a host body!

Your soul selects a human body for itself and breathes life into it during birth, and exits it at the time of death, in order to complete your spiritual *Karma* in a psychical body.

After death, your soul exits the body and begins its journey back 'home' to *God / The Creation*. You are eternal.

The life of the soul can also continue after death in parallel worlds or universes. There is a limited quantity of souls in the Universe. Each soul is divided into shrapnel of souls, which can be reincarnated parallel at the same planet or other planets, or even in parallel universes.

Life cannot be stopped:

You cannot destroy anything in the entire Universe, but you can change the aggregation mode and the energy state of the materials.

Each tree or blade of grass you uproot, every leaf or fruit that you pluck - will grow again.

Every forest you burn down, every lake or sea you pollute - will eventually renew itself.

Each planet that dissipates or explodes in space - will simultaneously create the seeds of stardust out of which new stars will be created.

The Universe and the stars expand and contract all the time like an eternal process of inhaling and exhaling. Everything is dynamic in endless cyclicality.

❧The right to die ❧

Everything that ends – had chosen to end.

Every person who died – his soul chose it.

No one should be forced to continue living!

Every soul, choose its moment of birth and death!

You must not prevent a person from ending his own life

You must not incarcerate and drug a person with medication in order to "preserve his life" while his soul is no longer interested in being in the body it selected.

When a person asks to end his life, it is important to listen to him, understand his motives and to advise him to choose different path without forcing him but allowed him to die in a dignified way based on his free will.

It is the right of every soul to end its journey
at any given moment, in order to attain
a new life and to start over.

Birth and death

In order for the soul to enter the body of a fetus (birth), always another soul must exit another body (death).

The birth of one person is the death of another.

That is the way both states must be celebrated:
At the time of birth, we celebrate the entry of the soul into the body.
At the time of death, we celebrate the departure of the soul from the body.
The souls came to Earth in order to have emotional experiences, to correct Karmas from previous incarnations and to testify the nature of themselves and by that : the nature of *God / The Creation.*

All knowledge is taught by studying its opposite. In other words:

- How can you appreciate light? unless you have experienced darkness.

- How will you know to appreciate success? unless you have experienced failure.

- How can you appreciate money or family? unless you have lost them.

- How can you appreciate love? until you have experienced loss or disappointment.

- How can you appreciate life? unless you lose the life of others or lose the part of your bodily functions.

❧ The 4 stages of death ❧

1. The first stage: Exiting the body

- The soul as a spirit **separates itself** from the body and the ego.

- **The soul looks at the body** from the outside and realizes that it's experiencing 'death', much time with a sense of confusion until the soul realizes that it is no longer dwells inside the body but separated from it.

- **The soul is been asked** by *'The Creation'*: If it is her final wish, whether to return back to the physical body or to leave it and continue its journey. *God / The Creation* will never take life without the soul's permission.

- If the soul **chooses to return** to the body it left, it will be sucked back into the body and will experience physical pain during the process.

2. The second stage: The corridor of light

Here the soul will experience tremendous frequency of love and must seek to find 'the corridor of light' without fear.

As the soul enters *'the corridor of light'*, someone there will be waiting for it: a relative, friend or any other person the soul chooses to meet. This depends on the constellation of **faiths**, which the soul has accumulated during its life as a spirit in a body:

If you believe in reincarnation – this is what you will experience. You will be able to watch and see parts of your previous incarnations and realize who you were in your past life.

If you believe that relatives and loved ones that have passed away will be waiting for you – then this is what you will experience.

If you believe that a spiritual or religious entity or even aliens will arrive to greet you – then this is what you will experience.

If you believe that you will meet *God / The Creation* will come to greet you– then this is what you will experience.

If you believe that you deserve to be punished and to suffer for your misdeeds in 'Hell'– then this is what you will experience.

If you believe that you were a good person and deserve to reach 'Heaven'- then this is what you will experience. 'Hell and Heaven' only exist in your head.

If you do not believe in *God / The Creation* - then you wi not notice it even after your death, in the same way, you di not notice it during your life. You will skip this stage and immediately be transferred to the third stage.

3. <u>The third stage: self-judgment without ego</u>

As the soul reaches the gates of 'heaven', it gives itself a 'fai trial' in front of the representatives of *'The creation'* and **without an ego the soul judges itself:**

"What have you done during your life inside a body?

How have you helped yourself and others and what contribution have you left behind?

What have you learned, what education or insights have you acquired for yourself?

What destiny and Karma have you achieved?"

God / The Creation is all love therefore, there *is no "wrath and fury of God" or "Chariots of the Gods",* those are superstitions from folk tales that were born out of the need to control people by intimidation.

4. <u>The fourth stage: Unification</u>

The soul still experiences a tremendous frequency of love on its way 'back home' to be unified with *God / The Creation*. The moment the soul reaches the end of its spiritual journey inside a living body, then it will spiritually ascend and will achieve **'enlightenment'**. The soul can choose to inhabit another living body or remain as a spirit and become a spiritual entity' it depends on its level of the 'spiritual hierarchy' it's had reached and the soul's free will.

❧ Return from death ❦

There are cases in which the soul choose to have a second chance:
At the time of death, the soul undergoes the first stage.
In the second stage, the soul is asked whether it chooses to return to the body or to continue on as a spirit.
If the soul elects at that stage to return to the body it inhabited, then it will quickly be sucked back into the body as a spirit and will experience a physical pain.

Clinical death

More than once. various people have experienced clinical death when their souls exit their body. Miraculously, each person gave a different description of an experience. It because **they had visited their 'own state of being' they had created for themselves.**

❧ Suicide ❧

The first rule is freedom of choice. *God / The Creation* wil never interfere with your choices.

In the same way that you can choose to be born, you are also allowed to choose to die, to end your journey as a spi inside a living body.

Your lives were lent to you in the same way that a book is borrowed from the library. You decide when you will retur it to the *"library of The Creation"*.

- People who choose to commit suicide, after death their soul returns *'home'* to the sources and will be surrounde by love and will never be abandoned or "be sent to hell" i they did not ask for it.

- Such people chose to let go of their lives after a tremendous spiritual or physical ordeal, which made it difficult for their soul to cope with a spirit inside a humar body on Earth.

- Such souls have suffered enough therefore, God / *The Creation* doesn't punish them again but love them with deep understanding and allows them, only if they want, t experience again in their next incarnation, in order to finish their *karma.*

They will need to experience the same difficult *karma* lesson in another life and body, in the infinite vastness of the Universe or on Earth; it all depends on the choices these people will make as souls.

- Sometime they may need to undergo thousands of incarnations, until they complete their *karma* task, have learned their lesson and achieved their destiny. In order to do so, they will continue to be reborn.

You should not judge harshly people who have chosen to commit suicide and avoid judging or disrespecting them.

For example (in the Jewish religion): do not bury them outside the "official boundary" of the cemetery as if they were 'unwanted trash'.

❧ Coma ❧

A Coma is a state, in which the soul is temporarily separated from the living body. The soul exists in the spiritual dimension (heavens) and the bod exists in the physical dimension (Earth).

During a coma, the soul discusses things with 'heavenly entities' and itself, whether to return to the physical body or detach itself and return 'home' to the source.

A person in a coma, will not experience any physical pain but his soul is aware of its state; hears and sees all that takes place around its physical body.

Which means, it might be that a person will be in a coma state for four years but in actuality, only "a few light hours" have passed up in the Universe.

When the soul leaves the body, then the pulse stops. Only
the soul decides for itself.

In-Universe there is no time,

 but darkness with few light spots.

Humanity invented time dimension,

which does not match the time in Heaven.

❧ Artificial respiration ❧

Connecting a sick or a coma patient to respiratory machines is done out of the genuine concern of his relatives and the medical staff to act according to their oath, to do everything in their power to extend life.

In order to make this dilemma easier to cope with, it is recommended to involve a spiritual medium or healer that can channel with the patient's soul, in order to receive information about him (which known to his loves ones) and to reveal if and what the patient decided.

During life, it's best to prepare a "living will" in which express your 'final life requests'.

The medical staff and the person's relatives must honor and comply with the person's request if he or she chooses not to be connected to the respiratory machines.

If the medical staff or the person's relatives do not grant the patient's request, they are **denying him the first rule** "freedom of choice" which is the freedom to choose to be born and when to die and at the same time they **activate the second rule** of 'All returns', such negative energy might return to the medical staff or the person's relatives and may restrict their 'freedom of choice' in their own life.

It is recommended that the doctor will also be a medium, just as Maimonides was a doctor as well as a medium. In order to combine the treatment of the physical body and combined with the soul.

The soul is responsible for producing diseases, pain, allergy or other symptoms, through them the source of the soul's frustration can be diagnosed.
"A healthy soul - in a healthy body".

The soul comes before the physical body

Euthanasia

Today, euthanasia is intended only for terminally ill patients in a few countries. There is no "mercy" in that because the medical staff is supposedly "doing a merciful act" which they are simply implements **the person's natural free will to die.**

A message to The Medical Staff:

"You who have been chosen to treat patients:

You must demonstrate patience, attentiveness, and care

respect people and their freedom of choice.

Do not burden them with examinations and medicine.

Use your emotional intelligence and intuition and

Use mediums and healers.

These sick souls seek for

assistance and spiritual redemption,

therefore their physical body is sick."

ꙮ Trapped souls ꙮ

There are cases, in which a soul leaves the body during death but for various reason, it cannot find or enter 'the corridor of light'. Such a soul is not certain of its decision: whether it should return to the body or leave it for good.

A soul that has left the physical body and not yet entered 'the corridor of light' therefore, **it still exists as a spirit** (ghost) and considered a 'trapped soul'. It is trapped in the '4 stages of death', between the spiritual dimension.

A trapped soul can often harass other souls that are in the physical or spiritual dimension and it does so out of fear, anger, frustration, and misunderstanding.

There should be help these trapped souls, in order to lead them to *'the corridor of light'*, so these souls can complete all '4 stages of death' and return to the source.

Question: "Why God doesn't help the trapped soul return' home' to him?"

Answer: "In all stages of death God / *The Creation* **continues to provides the free will to the soul** without interfering".

There are mediums who release trapped souls" and leading them into *'the corridor of light'*, allowing them to move forward.

❧ Heaven and Hell ❧

You cannot die. Death is a 'temporary station' in the soul's journey.

At the moment of death, the soul departs itself from the living body and from the ego and from that point every decision of the soul is pure.

If the soul realizes that it deserves to go to 'heaven' - that
what the soul will experience.

If the soul realizes that it has done wrong and deserve to b
'punished' and **sent to 'hell'** – that is what the soul will
experience.

**'Heaven and hell' do not exist in reality. They are not a
physical place but yet a state of a maid.**

**Thanks to the first rule "the free will" 'Heaven and hell'
look and seem different in the eyes of each soul.**

The moment you imagine – You create 'heaven or hell'
without ego.

- **When the soul reaches 'heaven',** it finds a place filled wi
  spectacular natural sights, infinite beauty and marvelous
  light, filled with love and happiness. Each soul will
  experience this place differently, according to its spiritua
  and energy level.

- **When the soul reaches 'hell',** it finds a darker place; the
  soul will be secluded and thinks about its errors in its
  previous incarnations and experiences a kind of spiritual
  suffering, but not actual physical suffering because a soul
  has no physical body which means that:

The soul will watch from the side and see itself
supposedly 'suffering' There it will understand its
mistakes so that it can choose wisely and make
corrections in its next incarnation. Each soul will

experience hell differently according to its spiritual and energetic progress.

The moment the soul realizes, that its stay in 'hell' is no longer meaningful and that there is no more need for it to 'suffer' then it will move on to the fourth stage of death and will merge with the source.

- Satan/the prince of darkness is not evil. He exists in order to allow free will for all souls in the infinite universe. Without him, there would be no possibility of choosing.

  There is no 'good and or evil' - everything is relative. This does not mean that 'heaven' is "good" and 'hell' is "bad".

- Darkness is not a state which exists in the absence of light! Darkness is a universal permanent state. The entire Universe exists in darkness Light is temporary and assists in the discovery of that which already exists in darkness.

The stars, the sun and the moon emit light without interruption throughout the day. The Earth turns on its axis and allows only half of the planet, every 12 hours, to be exposed to sunlight, in order to balance and provide humanity with darkness, a relief meant for sleep and relaxation. Perhaps a temporary stay in 'hell' is a necessary lesson for a soul which still did not learn its lesson and did not realize what mistakes it has made in previous incarnations. There are no coincidences, everything is always for the soul's benefit.

Darkness was here long before the light. The whole Universe exists in darkness. Light is intended for the discovery of that which already exists in darkness.

From the darkness, you were created and to the darkness, you shall return. Accept the darkness as a background color, upon which you shine, with the light of your souls.

The Five Earthly Senses

In the light, the five Earthly senses are active. they are activated in the physical dimension.

In the darkness, the five supernatural senses are active. they are not revealed in the physical dimension, but rather in the spiritual one. In order to experience these senses, you only need to shut your eyes and connect with the darkness.

Most people activate the five earthly senses through the physical body:

1. The sense of **touch**

2. The sense of **taste**

3. The sense of **smell**

4. The sense of **sight**

5. The sense of **hearing**

If you will add the word 'supernatural' to the abovementioned 'earthly senses' then you will get:

The five supernatural senses that are activated by the intuition sense which is been affected directly by the chakras and the auras:

1. The supernatural sense of **touch** (sensation)

2. The supernatural sense of **taste**.

3. The supernatural sense of **smell**

4. The supernatural sense of **sight**

5. The supernatural sense of **hearing**

Now you get the total of **Ten senses**.

All ten senses send knowledge vibrations

to the sense of intuition.

Those senses can be strengthened by

constant practice without fear.

It is amusing to call them 'unnatural senses',

when they are so natural and exist

within the intuition of every human being.

❧ Chapter 5 ❧

Burial

࿓ Death and birth ࿓

You cannot die.

Physical death is only a 'temporary stopover' on the soul's endless journey.

In order to walk the Earth, the soul must breathe life into a temporary physical body.

At the time of death, the soul departs from the physical body it inhabits and returns as a spirit back *'home'*. The only thing that the soul possesses is its freedom of choice! The physical body remains on Earth. It merely served as a vessel in which the soul dwelled during its life on Earth.

In birth - people prepare, rehearse and make arrangements. Sometimes they even hire the services of a childbirth instructor, who accompanies the entire process of pregnancy and birth.

In death - people avoid speaking about the subject or dealing with it out of fear and discomfort, but it must stop because death is final for every living human.

It is important to make 'death preparations'

with the help of an instructor

that explains, relaxes and prepares

the person for the moment of death.

Today, there are very few clinics that support and treat the terminally ill.

You must be rid of the fear of death by providing the right knowledge. Death is a part of the natural lifecycle of every living thing. In order for a soul to enter a fetus at the time of birth, another soul must leave a different body. Each moment of birth of one – is also a moment of death for other.

Do not fear death

The soul is a spirit that chooses to enter into a physical body on Earth, in order to correct itself, to ascend energetically and its higher purpose is to testify herself and The Creation.

At the time of death, when your soul departs from your body, you will feel an immense sense of relief, freedom and mainly the divine frequency of love.

If you enrich new insights then you will not fear death:

- You will not become a trapped soul. Such souls find it difficult to accept the fact that they are no longer inside a physical body; they are afraid to advance towards the light and remain trapped between the dimensions.

- You will know when to choose to die. Choose death at a time that's suitable for you. There are many people who suffer in their physical body but do not let go of it and remain to suffer in it, just because they are afraid of death.

This does not mean that you should commit suicide or take your own life!

God / The Creation will not be angry at you if you commit suicide, but it will not be in your favor because you will remain trapped in the same cyclical karma, it will haunt you again in your next incarnation, until you choose to rise above your difficulties and finish what you intended.

❧ Burial methods ❧

"Dust to dust and ashes to ashes..."

The physical body must return to the nature, should be cremated and less as buried in the ground. At the moment of death, it is highly important to save other lives by donated organs.

In most of Asia, the body is cremated. It's wise! In order to conserve land and avoid the need to bury dead bodies, since:

Most of the Earth is covered by water. This is why lands are a scarce resource and should be used by the living, not to bury the dead. At the end of the cremation ceremony, the ashes is scattered back into nature, according to the request of the deceased or his relatives.

In most of the developed countries, the body is buried in a plot of lands or in a walls, with a coffin and a gravestone above the grave.

This is NOT wise, because:

It is expensive and involves a waste of valuable land.

The grave might turn into a pilgrimage site, which is similar to idolatry.

"Thou shalt not make unto thee any graven image..."

Idolatry

Purchasing a burial spot involves considerable cost depending on: the location, type of stone and decorations, additions.

The moment the gravestone is placed on the burial spot, it officially becomes a pilgrimage site! Visiting the gravesite after a month and once every year after that, it is known as "the memorial passing day".

Each visit is a turned into a 'family event' which includes: inviting people, meals and gatherings, also eulogies and prayers with or without a member of the clergy (who usually charges a fee for his 'services').
This is also refers to the burial sites of 'holy' figures / places around the world. **Matter cannot be holy.**

Only the soul which gives life - is holy.

❧ Chapter 6 ❧

Health

✄ A migraine ✄

A migraine mostly affects women, because women come from the aliens, therefore they are more open to insights, innovations, and spirituality than men.

A migraine is a state which involves receiving information, channeling.

This channeling is received through the crown of the head (the crown chakra) then passes to the third eye (which is located between the eyebrows) and projects onto the sides the forehead. Physical symptoms include: pressure and pain which intensify until it finally subsides.

This is the reason migraines have no scientific explanation or cure. Every bodily phenomenon originates in the soul. Medicine cannot cure migraines but only to anesthetize the pain temporarily, because the origin of migraines is spiritual. Meditation and yoga can help reduce the stress.

How to deal with migraine

The moment the a migraine attacks, start writing and filling up pages, all that pops into your head. At first, only meaningless sentences will appear random thoughts and some undecipherable 'gibberish' until the main messages begin to appear. This will allow receiving the messages from 'The Creation' ,in order to release pressure and information which received in a channel.

∞Obsessive-Compulsive Disorder (O.C.D) ∞

This type of disturbance mostly affect people who are over-sensitive to their environment, with perfection thinking.

People with an O.C.D adopt rules and behaviors for themselves, in order to perform certain actions that will protect them and keep them sane from stress and flood of information.
They are afraid to lose their balance or to go mad. Some of their fears could be from their past incarnation.

The reason for this phenomenon:

This is not an inborn disturbance or a DNA problem but one that is acquired over the years and can affect anyone! This means that these people were not born with the disturbance but rather were drawn into it by:

- A crisis in their personal life, such as in their family or pressure at work

- Not being able to achieve a goal; having high standards and perfection that are difficult to meet.

- Lack of sleep, etc.

People who suffer from such a disturbance, have reached a crisis and a turning point in their lives following a traumatic event. Alternatively, people with O.C.D are constantly thinking destructive, bothersome and damaging thoughts without being able to release themselves, out of fear that "a disaster" will take place.

Their brain does not allow them to release such repeating actions and they enter into a circle, which is in their mind. **In order to help them, one must understand what happene in previous incarnations as well in the current incarnation, that affects them so horribly.**

Tip for reducing O.C.D:

Use a notebook, mobile phone or recording device and document each bothersome thought in it, including the time it appeared and the number of times it appeared.
The moment an action is performed - it should be documented, for example:

"I closed the door... and checked to see if it is closed; it is now 10:12."

"I washed my hands with soap at 15:10."

"A disturbing thought is currently passing through my mind... I will now describe it and document the time..."

Once it has been recorded - there is no need to repeat it.

** The abovementioned tip is by no means a medical prescription but a recommendation or an opinion. In case of any medical, mental or psychological problem, one should consult with the proper health care provider in order to receive treatment and counseling.

ও The mentally ill ৬

'A healthy soul - in a healthy body'.
The soul comes before the physical body, therefore **the source of the physical problem is in the soul and the spirit. Every pain in the soul – projected onto the physical body.**

People cannot be cured using only conventional medicine,

because the soul is the ones that "sick".

Medicine can only anesthetize, blur and remove

the problem temporarily but cannot fully cure it.

The mentally ill can hear voices and see images

because their halos are torn.

It is hard to believe the mentally ill because only they can see and hear their images. This is because the auras around them are torn and damaged.

Human beings are surrounded by seven halos, in order to balance and protect the body from the outside.

When halos are damaged and torn as a result of crisis and depression, then a person is losing his mental balance and he begins to experience most of his the ten senses, without any option for control or balance, because he doesn't have the tools to control the ten senses. Medicine can blur and temporarily soothe but it wouldn't solve the soul's distress

A message for Psychologists, Doctors, and Advisors

"Patients cannot be helped only by conversations

and medicine which are provided by professionals.

You do not understand the cause of the illness

because the source of the problem is – spiritual.

You will be able to discover that

only by using medium's help

or if you use your ten senses.

In order to understand the spirit (soul) you have to be a spirit man (medium). You can't cure only with medicine (matter) and conversations".

Sleep

During sleep the soul leaves the body in which it is imprisoned in order to rest and connect with the spiritual world, to which it belongs. When the soul leaves the body it is connected by a 'thin silver thread' to the navel. The soul's travels are translated into dreams and it returns to the body when the sleeping person awakens.

The moment you frighten or bother a sleeping person, you disrupt the level at which his spirit is located. This disturbance may cause fear, restlessness, even madness because while sleeping the soul is temporarily outside the human body.

This is why, it is not recommended to ask 'psychological or spiritual experts' to perform past life regression on those who are suffering from disturbances, mentally ill, etc.

The situation is delicate and dangerous for the person, by opening the previous incarnations, it might affect the subconscious to recall difficult and painful events from the past, memories that may cause great spiritual harm.

In order to help, it's recommend to use the ten senses or reach a medium or a spiritual person, who will check the source for the problem without telling all the vision's details.

Everything comes from the soul and the subconscious, this is where the memories of the past are accumulated, as well one's knowledge and talents.

Opening the chakras

There are those who turn to spiritual people and ask them "open their chakras" in an artificial way, like opening the third eye. This act is not recommended due the following:

- Opening the chakras artificially may activate the ten senses all at once rather than gradually, that might open the ability to hear voices, smell scents, and see visions, colors, deceased, aliens and entities, without any control

- Chakras that were opened - will not be able to close automatically but can only be closed by the person himse with the aid of spiritual people.

- The chakras are energetic circular muscles that can be opened and closed by the use of the imagination. In orde to close them, you should practice by imaging the chakra becoming smaller.

❧ illness ❦

illness at a young age: It is not uncommon that we encounter cases in which young children become ill and we can't help but wonder:

"Why was this child destined to have an illness, a child that did not commit any crime and has never sinned? It is unfair why is there no justice in the world?"

This difficult question usually remains unanswered. Following is a spiritual answer: The soul chooses all it life's pathways - both the difficult ones and the easy ones. A soul arrives as spiritual into a physical body on Earth in order to undergo lessons and corrections. It can choose to be born and become sick at an early age.

This happens so that a soul can understand and **appreciate anew the value of life**. That is to say, that **the soul of the young child did not appreciate life** in its previous incarnations, perhaps destroyed, killed, wounded, abused, committed suicide or controlled others and acted with kind of force and cruelty with no mercy and thus correct the lessons *(karma)* that it carries with it

In most cases, **it will choose to value the life** as it suffers from an illness, pain or defect only to ascend to a higher energy level of the soul.

*Sometimes the life of the soul within the physical body will be short. You cannot be born or die **unless you chose** to do so as a soul. God will not give you life or take it from you - unless you choose to ask for it.*

Remember: **you cannot die.**

Before the soul enters a human body in each incarnation, it chooses how it wants to correct it *karma* and lessons it did not manage to correct during its previous incarnations.

Each soul that leaves the body - returns 'home', it can choose to return and breathe life into a different body, whether on Earth / on other planets or remain as a spirit. Everything happens for the best. Human beings accumulate life experiences and insights from the suffering and hardships they underwent during each incarnation.

illness at an older age

All illness originates from the soul.

A person becomes ill because his soul his soul signals to him
the source of the problem.

Diseases are the result of erroneous life lessons that a perso
accumulated during his life. A person who grows up with
emotions and anger, adopts a problematic lifestyle, one that
involves toughness, nervousness, outbursts, impatience,
over-sensitivity, harming the environment, egoism and
hard-headedness, lack of trust and respect, jealousy, hatred
and self-destruction and In addition, some unhealthy
lifestyles too.

Such a person, who cannot find a cure for the pain in his
soul, might turn for lack of any other choice to addiction,
whether it be smoking, drugs, alcohol, food, hoarding, etc.

Each person is born with a natural healing capability,
whether by positive thinking or by sending healing energies
from the soul the body. Illnesses can usually be cured by a
combination of spiritual and physical healing.

The healing of the soul - can be accomplished by using all
ten senses. With the aid of a spiritual person/medium who
can spiritually diagnose the spiritual source of the problem.

Healing of the body - by consulting with a doctor who can
physically diagnose the cause of the person's illness. In the
future, there won't be general medications or vaccinations
but drugs adapted to DNA.

Today, the number of patients and hospitals around the globe is growing with every passing year. There are those who will say that this is "thanks" to the advanced technology. Indeed, technology has improved and advanced worldwide healthcare system and yet it has also introduced many problems, such as: the commercialization of worldwide medicine, intrigue, struggles, experiments on animals and human beings and more.

❧ Vaccinations ❦

Vaccinations which are not individual genetically adapted, may cause a defects in a younger ages or during lives.

It is true, that vaccinations for terrible diseases had prevented disease and death mainly with the mankind's industrialization

Vaccinations are still provided to all without any first medical examination. Because each human body is different from the other. It affect children and adults.

Children might get deformities, childhood diseases, autisms and allergy symptoms and it also includes adults who are receiving vaccine.

In order to avoid these risks, before receiving a vaccine, you must require performing a medical DNA adopt examination to all living form (that include people, animals and pesticide any plans) and only then to receive a DNA suited custom vaccination.

❧ Chapter 7 ❧

Life & Soul

✌ Life ✌

- It is **a great privilege** for the body to awaken when t soul breathed life into it.

- In the same way that the black hole is cyclical and eternal, the souls are endless. Everything around us alive and eternal. You cannot permanently disappear kill or destroy anything on earth or in the entire universe. **You can change the modes of aggregation of material but do not eliminate anything.**

- **Life is the only sacred thing.** Not books, nor rocks, n people or religions. **Nothing is sacred except the sou**

- In order to be born or to die – the soul must choose t do so! *God / The Creation* will not take life without the soul agreeing to it and requesting him to do so. **Only the soul make the decision** whether to continue to dwell in a body and breathe life into it or to leave **i**

- **The mission of all souls in the living body** is to testify about themselves and to correct and thus to testify about the nature of *God / The Creation*

- Each system has many planets. **Humans can exist onl on one planet in each system**. In the solar system, humans can live only on planet Earth.

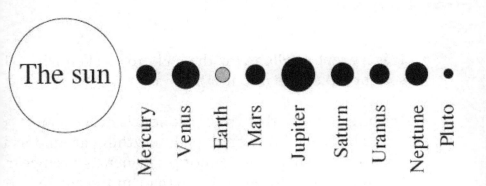

Black holes

There are countless black holes in the Universe. They are different from one another in location and size. The solar system including planet Earth is located inside a black hole. The black hole is the basis for the energy dynamics of living systems in the Universe. There is a constant flow of energy inside a black hole, which is emitted outward and then return it.

The Solar System, the planets, the galaxies, the biological cell, the atoms, the molecules, the human body and the process of breathing: inhalation and exhalation as the Universe's expansion, they're all connect together.

❧ The Soul ❦

- When a newborn baby takes its first breath - only then **the soul enters the body**.

There cannot be a situation in which two souls occupy the body of a single pregnant woman during pregnancy.

- A soul activates the wondrous machine of the human body. The fetus in its mother's womb is soulless. The soul enters the body of the fetus only during birth when it takes its first breath. The fetus feeds and breathes through its mother, through the umbilical cord. A fetus is not considered to be an independent entity. Without the umbilical cord, it would not survive. This is why an abortion should not be viewed as murder because the soul has not yet entered the body of the fetus.

- The soul does not have an ego. At the moment the soul enters a living body, it receives ego for survival purpose.

- The soul is in every living thing: in the air, water, plants, animals and human beings.

  The soul can choose to breathe life into a body or to remain a spirit. The soul moves on the axis of light, between an endless variety of galaxies, worlds, and parallel universes, in the infinite space of the Universe. Think big.

- Spirit has no beginning and no end. The time that the soul stays in each body is short, compared to its infinite lifetime as a spirit.

- The moment of death is joyous and liberating for the soul, which was trapped inside the body. Every physical death is a transit station from the material to the spirit.

During sleep

The soul experiences freedom when the body is sleeping. It left the body, attached to the navel with a thin silver cord. It hovers as a spirit in parallel worlds, travels through time, and then returns to the body before it awakes.

This is why one must not scare a sleeping person. It may cause him trauma up to rifts in his auras, fears, memory problems and concentration, and even madness.

Prolonging life

You cannot die. You are eternal.
You can always elect to naturally reincarnate as a spirit or inside a physical body.

Prolonging life artificially in hospitals against a person's wishes goes against the first rule 'the freedom of choice'.

The right thing to do:

1. If a person is <u>not</u> in fully conscious (coma): then until he regains consciousness, to choose whether to continue living inside the body or not, he will be connected to artificial respiration only if he asked for during his life. without the artificial equipment, the soul would leave the body without a pulse.

2. Each person must prepare for himself during his life: a 'final life requests'.

3. If the person is fully conscious and asks to leave his bod
due to a severe illness or from any other personal reaso
then he could choose whether to live or end his life.

It is wise to advise to a person who wishes to die and to
provide him consultation, but not to decide for him becaus
it will delete his free will and then the second rule 'All
returns' is automatically activated as *karma*, and returns
back to those are responsible for not allowing him to act
according to his free will.

People who ask that their lives be ended:

In most cases, those people also chose to end their lives in
their previous incarnations and they carry with them ancie
karma that will be released in the moment they achieve
their goal during their lifetime. Such people, whose soul ha
requested to leave their bodies, will choose to get a new life
each and every time, whether in a body or in spirit until
their soul reaches 'enlightenment' in a living body and then
it returns 'home' to merge with *God / The Creation*.

In spite of a human being's free will – **it is not recommende
that people commit suicide,** because the act in itself does n
solve the main problem, which will become a 'karma
problem' which mean that the soul will enter a spiritual loo
and will continue to reincarnate with the same problem,
until it finds some way to deal with fears, accomplish and to
learn its lesson.

This can be demonstrated in the following way:
If a person tries to pass a driving test and fails, it will not help him to kill himself.
He will need to keep trying (reincarnate in an endless loop) until he faces his problem (*karma*), solves it (the correction) and successfully passes the driving test.

❧ The book of life ❧

- In the Big Bang, a single soul and a single planet exploded and were scattered as dust and replicate themselves throughout the Universe. This is how the planets and souls were created.

- The quantity of souls in the Universe is limited. You cannot give birth endlessly. In order for a soul to enter the body of a fetus (birth), another soul must exit a different body (death).

The travels of the soul (past-present and future) although there is only present in the Universe. All it journey is documented in the *Book of Life* which located in the **Universal Cosmic Library,** for example: what are the soul's main and second lifelines, in which bodies it dwelled in and for how long, in which period of the human history and in which roles, from what it had suffered, in which family it was born, its talents, it destiny and which lessons.

With the aid of a Medium, spiritual tools or deep meditation, you can ask the soul or the accompanying 'spiritual guide' to provide and reveal you with some spiritual messages, information, and answers from your *Book of Life*.

Not all the information from your *Book of Life* will be give
to you, in order not to confuse, maintained curiosity and fr
will.

ꙮ A Spiritual guide ꙮ

You are not alone on Earth. Each soul in a physical body ar
every living being has a spiritual guide.

The role of the spiritual guide is to provide guidance and
security regarding decisions in life. *'The creation'* **provides
this spiritual guidance for every living body that contains a
soul on the face of the Earth.**

The soul begins its incarnations on the face of the Earth,
according to the following ladder of spiritual hierarchy:

As a plant, an animal, human being, alien, entity of light.

The soul's travels can go up or down the spiritual ladder;
therefore in your current incarnation you can be as a human
being, and in your next ones you could be an animal or a
plant, according to your lessons which you have to learn.

Spiritual guides change in each period of time. In most case
when the guides change, the person will be in a state of
uncertainty, loneliness, depression, etc.

The spiritual guide does not necessarily know you from
previous or current incarnations. A spiritual guide might be

a departed family member even from way back, a friend from the past, an acquaintance, a historical or religious figure.

A spiritual guide avoids from revealing himself to human, especially because it might scare rather than help them.

❧ Past life regression ❧

Each person has a subconscious, where all the information about his previous incarnations is collected and stored in the *Book of Life*. The subconscious remembers everything.

The conscious part of the brain represses the past incarnations in order that we can remain balanced and not go insane from 'remembering' our past incarnations (which some were good and others not) and to allow us a fresh start to choose and correct without feelings of guilt.

When people are afraid or feeling threatened by something in their lives - it means that their subconscious 'remembers' a similar encounter from a previous incarnation, an encounter which has left its mark of trauma, fear, and frustration that hunt them even now.

1. In the same way, when people feel an attraction and attachment to certain people, interests, professions, places, etc. this means that their subconscious 'remembers' a similar encounter of attraction from a previous incarnation. There are no coincidences!

2. 'All the incarnations that each person has undergone, difficult and cruel incarnations from his past incarnations, which the soul prefers to 'forget', are stored in the

subconscious and in that book so as not to burden a man's daily existence. That is why **past life regression is not recommended,** because:

1. You can't correct those images from your current or previous incarnations, but only can change your perspective and understand that all were happened for a short period and for your own good.

2. These professionals do not have the knowledge and the ability, similar to a spiritual person or Medium, to look forward and backward in time and understand.

Past life regression must be done by a medium or high-level of spiritual professional, who can receive information and provide only the relevant and useful information without reconstructing the events or 'carry' the patient back in time with him. It could be a very risky game which may leave fears and traumas in the patient.

"That which is hidden from you

in the subconscious – you must not touch.

There is a divine higher purpose that

prevents you from remembering

in order to protect and allow you

to make a new choice each time".

Past life regression may cause more harm than good to the patient's soul.
Even if it's made by spiritual professional, a patient which is under hypnosis or undergoes a guided imagery process, and "succeeds" in seeing himself in past incarnations which can involve disturbing imagery: killing, self-suffering or causing suffering, wounding, abusing others, that could disrupt the balance and tranquility of his soul and bring on a trauma.

The right thing to do is:
To turn to a highly-skilled spiritual person or a Medium who can see the patient's incarnations and provide with answers to: What is the source of the fears? Why does he repeat on the same mistakes? What to correct in his life? All is done to assist them in making corrections without unnecessary burdens on energy levels.

☙ Karma ❧

The interpretation of the word 'karma':

- In Sanskrit *'karma'* mean: **refers to the spiritual principle of cause and effect to every action.**

- *Karma* is negative energy that the soul carries with it, from its previous incarnations into its current incarnation, which it did not fully complete yet. **Karma is the Energetic engine which leads and pushes the soul to fulfill and correct itself from one incarnation to the next.**

- Every human being is born with *karma*. All the harmful actions a person performed in his previous incarnations create *karmas* for him that he must correct anew in each life.

- If the soul will not finish the test, for which it arrived in its current incarnation, then it will repeat the same test i its next incarnation, until it completes the test and ascends to a new energy level, like in a game.

- There are no coincidences. Each person whom you have met, fallen in love with, were hurt by or had an argumen probably is known to you from your past incarnations! And your soul has chosen to reincarnate with that perso again, in order to finish karma issues that were not successful in the past.

Most cases of murder, killing, crime, suicide, etc. are th result of negative *karma*, which the soul carries with from past incarnations and repeats the same mistak because it did not yet achieve a correction.

The moment the soul finishes the karma, then it will hav reached a 'correction' and will not need to reincarnate again with that same person or issue in its future incarnations.

In order to complete its 'correction', a soul does not nee to forgive and love every person or issue in each and every incarnation, BUT must feel complete without negative feelings about those people or events.

Karma Cleansing

Medical problems are originated from the wounded soul. The soul is the entity that determines the health of the body.

Karma cleansing involves a person's option to clean and disconnect karmas and negative energies from his past incarnations.

Karma cleansing can be done in the following way:

1. Imagine the troubling person or issue, standing in front of you, face to face, with the umbilical cord connecting, is between you.

2. Imagine you holding a sharp instrument, cutting the umbilical cord in the middle.

3. Half of the cut umbilical cord will be absorbed within each body, which means that half of the umbilical cord will be absorbed into your body and the remaining half into the other person or issue.

4. Wrap the troubling person or issue with a white bubble of light or any other color and ask the troubling person or the issue to turn around and start walking, until it becomes a tiny dot of light on the horizon. This can be repeated several times until you feel a relief and change.

✜ Chapter 8 ✜

Auras and chakras

ᕎ Auras ᕬ

Every living body has auras that protect and balance it:

7 auras surround the body

Their purpose: to preserve and protect from **the outside.**

7 chakras are within the body

Their purpose: to preserve and balance **from within.**

An aura is an electro-energetic field which surrounds every living creature. Each field has a different strength and frequency vibration which can be measured.

Every energy field is directly influenced by the physical, emotional, spiritual and mental state of the living creature. All of these affect the clarity, wholeness, size, shape, and color of the aura.

The colors of the auras are indications of the person's personality, behavior patterns, reactions, inner consciousness, etc.

Types of auras

Following are descriptions of auras, from the inside to the outside of the body:

1. The physical aura - the first aura, the closest to the physical body.
2. The etheric aura - is located second.
3. The emotional aura - is located third.
4. The mental aura - is located fourth.
5. The causal /intuitive aura - is located fifth.
6. The spiritual (karma) aura - is located sixth.
7. The divine aura - is located seventh and last.

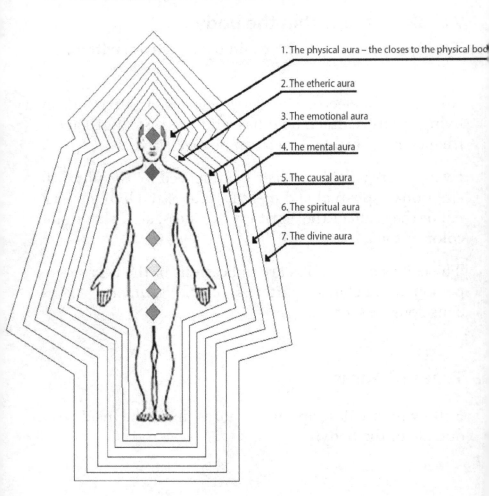

The meaning of the aura's colors

Today, technological instruments are able to photograph a living body and obtain data from it, through perspiration, pulse, and heat. Such details provide information about electromagnetic energy and electrical resistance and are processed and translated into the colors of the real-time energies and auras and then transferred to a computer screen. Each color has its own meaning:

Blue: Imagination and inspiration, giving, channeling, intuition, making peace, serenity, sensitivity, worry, loneliness, sadness, memory problems and inner strife.

Green: Care and sympathy, honesty and support, tranquility and sensitivity to the environment, implies miserliness, jealousy, suspiciousness, lack of care and the lack of confidence.

Purple: Spirituality, supernatural eyesight, care, leadership, independence, humility, wisdom, a tendency toward belligerence, control and coercion.

Pink: Love, pampering, sensitivity, compassion, care, friendship, tranquility, humility, beauty, implies dissatisfaction, jealousy, distrust and the lack of confidence.

Red: Energy, joy, love, passion, sexuality, self-confidence and creativity, illness, inflammation, nervousness, jealousy, distrust, and moodiness.

Yellow: Wisdom, learning, renewal, care, hate, optimism, and creativity.

Orange: Pride, vanity, incitement, criticism, and distrust.

Brown: The color of earth, the source of growth, communication, care, loneliness, vulnerability, secrecy, and illness.

Silver: Healing, spirituality, compassion, fertility, a high level of creativity, implies disinterest, and materialism.

Gold: Healing, inspiration, energy and spiritual enlightenment, disinterest in others, egotistic, materialism, and jealousy.

Black: Implies a frightened individual who needs protection and assistance in life. At the edges of the auras, there could be holes and cracks that appeared in the auras following a crisis, illness, addiction or abuse.

White: The white color contains all colors, just like in a prism. It reflects purity, creativity, truth, good-heartedness, enlightenment, insight and a high level of communication.

࠾ Chakras ࠾

The word chakra means a spinning wheel. The chakras exi
in all living creatures.

The human body has seven main energy centers that are
connected to the central body lines. From the upper part, i.
the crown of the head, to the lower part, i.e. the tailbone
which is at the end of the spinal column.

Between these main energy centers, numerous secondary
chakra centers are connected inside the physical body and
between the auras. Those points are used in Acupuncture.

**Each main chakra is responsible for a different layer of the
body and they are all working together in order to create
balance in a human body.**

Each chakra is associated with different parts of the physica
body, with a different color and sound and all chakras
together contain the seven colors of the rainbow:

Red, orange, yellow, green, blue purple and white. As like ir
a prism, they are all composed of the spectrum's colors and
are arranged by wavelength.

All seven colors merge into the pure white color of the sou

Types of chakras

The following are descriptions of the chakras, from the lowest to the highest:

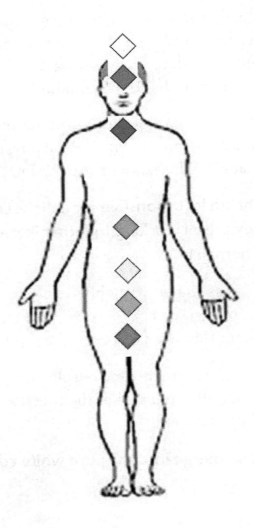

1. Red - The Root Chakra

Base chakra, located in the tailbone.
Responsible for the survival instinct, financial success, procreation. It is the source of inspiration and wishes.
Controls the bodily functions of the kidneys, the pituitary gland, lower spine, and feet.
Symptoms indicating that it is blocked: fear, pressure, concern, stubbornness, a desire to struggle and fight, violent tendencies that result from insecurity.

2. Orange - The Sacral Chakra

Located in the pelvis (three fingers below the navel).
Responsible for sexuality and creativity, interpersonal relationships, procreation, courage, fear, desire and passion.
Controls the bodily functions of the spleen, sexual organs, and back.
Symptoms indicating that it is blocked: restlessness and a lack of concentration, problems with: interpersonal relationships, sexuality, fertility, kidneys, bladder, and lower back.

3. Yellow - The Solar Plexus Chakra

Located in the diaphragm area, above the navel.

Responsible for the sense of inner strength, sensations, fears, desires and emotions, such as: hatred, anger, jealousy, and depression. When you scare a person, his stomach is the first area that reacts and 'jumps'.

Controls the bodily functions of the liver, pancreas, spleen, gall bladder, nervous system, and psychosomatic problems.

Symptoms indicating that it is blocked: dissatisfaction, sadness, moodiness, frustration, nervousness, ego, frustration and depression, Problems with blood pressure, intestines, stomach.

4. Green - The Heart Chakra

Located above the heart, at the center of the chest.
It is the central body chakra, which separates the 3 upper chakras and the 3 lower ones and **balances the whole body.**

Responsible for love, compassion and a sense of forgiveness.

Controls the bodily functions of the circulatory & respiratory systems, lungs, thymus gland, immune & lymphatic systems.

Symptoms indicating that it is blocked: anger, moodiness, nervousness, stubbornness, and dissatisfaction.
Problems with: blood flow, blood pressure, diabetes, capillaries, asthma, immune system, lymphatic system.

5. Blue - The Throat Chakra

Located at the base of the throat.

Responsible for Self-expression & interpersonal communication.

Controls the bodily functions of the thyroid, neck, throat, vocal chords, communication, and self-confidant.

Symptoms indicating that it is blocked: thyroid, stuttering criticism, being judgmental, oversensitivity, perfectionism, cynicism, and hoarseness, a tendency to catch colds, acute pharyngitis and neck stiffness.

6. Purple - The Third Eye Chakra

Located in the middle of the forehead, between the eyebrows.

Responsible for clear eyesight, channeling and sensory perception, intuition, deep understanding, ability to imagine and fulfill thoughts and ideas. An ability to develop the ten senses.

Controls the bodily functions of eyes and ears, and the sleep

Symptoms indicating that it is blocked: poor eyesight and hearing, head and ear aches, problems with: eyes, migraines an inability to fall asleep, nightmares and inner struggles that result from a lack of self-awareness.

7. White - The Crown Chakra

Located at the crown of the head.

The white color contains all 7 colors of the rainbow as a prism.

Responsible for receiving information and analyzing data from the Universe, channeling abilities.

Controls the bodily functions of the pineal gland, upper brainstem, right forehead and right eye.

Symptoms indicating that it is blocked: depression, isolation, lack of caring, a superficial view of the world and an inability to experience dimensions beyond physical reality.

❧ Chapter 9 ❧

Preparations for the Aquarius Age

❧ The year 1945 ❧

Following World War I, *God / The Creation* decided to intervene in the events on Earth, to prevent self-destruction by creating a *chaos* and selecting the element of destruction which was: World War II by Hitler and his allies. **The motive was to accelerate the process towards the entrance of the new Aquarius Age (which will begin in the year 2106) by an acceleration of technology.**

The result was a period of *chaos*, in which millions of people were killed all over the world, in order to allow more enlightened souls to enter and populate the Earth.

As each war filled with ego and male stubbornness there were no winners or losers, all sides suffered from death and destruction. Politics was invented in a purpose of preventing unnecessary wars.

The number of souls in the Universe is limited. In order to bring a soul into the world (birth) then another one must be exit it (death). Death is the passage of the soul from body to spirit or from spirit to spirit. All souls are eternal and endlessly continuous. So no one really dies in world wars, all souls are eternal and occasionally choose to inhabit a body for a short period

When the soul leaves the body, the deceased no longer suffers physically and it is possible to keep communicating with the deceased's soul, but only if the soul wishes to.

Each creation begins with chaos

Creation sets targets – in order to recreate

Chooses the element of chaos and destruction

Allows that element to create death and destruction

Annihilates the element of destruction

Finishes an age / era.
Many souls finish their bodily lives

Opens a new age and brings in enlightened souls

World War II

World War II was a result of the frustration of the Germa
nation which had been defeated by the French in World
War I and suffered from massive unemployment and a sen:
of frustration. This brought about the rise of the Nazi part
which was led by Hitler.

Hitler was chosen by *The Creation* to bring on *chaos* in
order to create. chose to demonstrate to future generations
that hatred only brings destruction.
The Nazis took pride in being "an improved race" that
superior to all others. They established a ruthless
totalitarian regime that took out its frustrations on the
weakest levels of society, such as: The foreigner and the
weak, the Jews, the Gypsies and the disabled, those who ha
different sexual tendencies and regime resistors.
The Nazis actively chose to destroy all that interfered with
or threatened them. In order to accomplish this, the
Germans used the following measures:

- Brainwashing through forceful speeches and conventions
  all carried out in the most educated, intellectual and
  intelligent.

- They used prisoners for building gas chambers, ghettos,
  railroad tracks, roads, concentration, and death camps, it
  was with the intention of imprisoning and killing their
  citizens of Germany and citizens from other conquered
  countries.

- Purchase and manufacture of: medical, technological and industrial equipment, cyanide gas, ovens for crematoriums, vehicles, weapons, etc.

World War II came to emphasize the fact that:

Ruin and destruction can result from brainwashing, not only in barbarian and cultureless populations but also in most cultured populations as the Germans. The German population was elegant, intellectual and cultured, possessed an advanced scientific technology and an awareness to preserve nature and the environment. Due to this regime which brought to environment destruction:

World War II was caused by *The creation* in order to finish one era and begin a better one. Vast areas in Germany, throughout Europe and Japan, were bombed and destroyed.

Following the second rule ('All returns') Berlin was divided to two after the war for fear that the 'Nazi snake' might strike again. One part was governed by the United States and the other was by Russia (until 1989). This division affected and divided the German society.

Many Nazi seniors, were committed suicide, caught and put on trial or escape to distant countries as Hitler did, under false identities. Hitler's death was forged with the body of a burned woman. He fled with Eva Brown to Argentina and lived there on an isolated island, for about 8 years until he died from various diseases.

Hitler

Hitler was chosen by 'the creation' to cause chaos in order recreate a new era, to start a war and bring destruction to Europe and around the world. There were many who opposed Hitler, tried to assassinate him and bring his rule an end, they were all unsuccessful in spite of all the attempts. Hitler felt he was a protected "divine messenger" that no one could harm.

The German nation was chosen by 'the creation' because it is considered to be meticulous, well-organized and love perfection. It is a nation that documents every piece of information in documents, written plans, films and so forth we need to "thank" them for that detailed historical documentation of World War II that exists to this day.

In the year 1945, *The creation* annihilates the element of destruction (Hitler) once its 'role' was finished.

Many still think that Hitler took his own life, but the truth is that Hitler escaped with Eva Braun to Argentina using submarine and de died there from illnesses after 8 years, where he lived as a prisoner on an isolated island.

Let's not forget another horrible dictator named Stalin, the Russian ruler at the time. He established a cruel and tyrannical regime, which abolished human rights, imprisoned and executed millions of Russian citizens, including ideological rivals, in work camps and prisons.

World War II took the lives of more than 50 million, In order t reinvent themselves in technologically upgraded and compassionate souls.

Try for a moment to comprehend just part of the picture, for example, that:

The number of Russians casualties was about 20 million.

The number of German casualties was about 10 million.

The number of Jewish casualties was about 6 million.

The souls of these millions of victims were chosen in advance to come into the world for a limited amount of time in a purpose of closing one era and begin a new one.

You cannot die. Those souls have earned the privilege of being reborn in a new body in their next incarnation or to remain spirits, according to what they have chosen afterlife.

❧ The New Age children ❧

Those who were born since 1945 onwards are mostly souls of 'The New age's children'.

After the destruction of World War I, 'the creation' decided to establish order and reorganization in the world. In order to reorganize - *chaos* must first be produced. All the participants were chosen in advance, from Hitler to the last of the participants including the victims.

As an eternal soul, no one can die. The number of souls is limited, so in order to bring new souls into the world, others must exit from Earth.

Those souls are *'The New Age children'* that have:

Much higher cognitive abilities, technological, patience, and curiosity, which their souls came from distant planets: The Indigo Children and The Crystal Children.

Both came to reducing the gap between planets in the universe while we are entering the Aquarius Age in the year 2106 (read my second book: The Future, Lucy 2018)

The indigo children

Were born since the year 1945 onwards:

The Indigo Children came to <u>advance the technology</u>.

These children have ancient and exalted souls that in most cases **arrived from distant planets in order to help advance innovation, technology and improve the quality of life**.

They are inventors; they are considered to be sensitives, geniuses, very talented and competitive souls with a sharp analytical mind, in several domains, such as hi-tech, science and medicine, aviation, etc.

Some of them cannot find a common language with the environment. As part of their destiny and correction, they have arrived to learn about emotions. Thanks to them, technological progress will be accelerated much faster than we experience today.

The crystal children

Were born since 1970 onwards:

The Crystal Children came <u>to unify the social humanity and to change the world education system</u>, The ADHA children.

Their source is from distant planets, as souls, they are new here on Earth and this is why they are more curious (because everything is new to them).

In the same way that a crystal is clear and does not hide anything, that's how they are real, honest and do not hide anything. Some of them don't like to speak much and other love to fight for the community, rights, and justice.

During the Pisces Age (The Future, Lucy 2018) men have caused destruction on Earth and always from ego and financial reasons.

Therefore, *The creation* has decided to bring higher souls to Earth, a new generation who cares and will change a lot in favor of nature, animals, human environment, social communication and global union, while we are entering the Aquarius Age in the year 2106.

They are considered to be: spiritual, stubborn, rebellious and impatient, they love adventure, music, and water, travel, changes, experiences and have an urge to seek new experiences, learn and actively change things. Most of them have almond eyes and a penetrating gaze that can read other people's thoughts. They love being outdoors. Their principles are "live and let live" and "respect and appreciate the environment".

The crystal children usually activate all 10 senses. Their brain waves actually operate in a different way, for exampl they can hear or see from afar.

Because of their needs in constant curiosity, they are fearless, easily influenced by tremendous physical force. It is recommended that they are protected and be given clearly defined boundaries so that they won't turn to destructive ways from within their ceaseless curiosity.

Also, it is recommended that they are challenged socially and physically in order to strengthen their sense of responsibility and their relationship with the environment.

They are not intended to violence but can become violent out of distress in cases in which the environment does not understand, respect and assist them in fulfilling their destiny.

The crystal children came to:

1. To preserve, protect and heal the Earth; to teach the res of humanity about emotions, caring, and tolerance.

2. To change the global education system. These children are classified as ADHA. The education system does not understand them because it lacks the necessary financial means, openness to innovation and mostly tolerance. To bring about far-reaching educational change, some of which has already been achieved, such as smaller classes, individualized or outside learning, coaching, remedial teaching, etc. All those good things were achieved thank to them.

The 60s'

Take those who were born in the year 1945 and add to them 15 years, then you'll reach the year 1960. This is the enlightened generation of the 'flower children' (indigo and crystal children) who sought to bring light, peace, and love, to change the government's priorities, accept other and improve for future generations as "make love, not war."

They were able to bring about positive change, for example the US withdrew from Vietnam, laws that discriminate against African-Americans were abolished (thanks to the enlightened leader Martin Luther King) and equal rights for men and women were achieved and much more.

They left their mark on the field of technology as well, a field that has developed rapidly since then. Mention the pioneers of the biggest hi-tech inventors: Bill Gates – Microsoft, Steve Jobs – Apple, IBM, Google, Facebook, etc.

ॐॐ

A license to have children and educate them

Bringing children into the world is not part of a person's destiny but only a humans survival need. The law of the global government supervision will require a license from all human being for having children, as we reached a state of overpopulation.

Having children is not a 'religious edict' or destiny.
It's not a duty to have children.
Human beings decide to have children for
egotistical reasons, fearing they will get older alone.

Only adults who choose to become parents and to create a
nuclear family for themselves will be able to do so provided
they have been trained and have received 'a government
license' which permits them to bring children into the world

To receive a license will require undergoing a process that
involves training, examinations, tests both physiological and
mental health assessments conducted by professional
institutes that will be composed of doctors, medical advisor
highly spiritual men and women, social works and
government representatives (without psychologists).

A license to have children will be given in exactly the same
way as other types of licenses: to drive, to practice law or
medicine or in order to build.

In the current situation:

Overpopulation - today there are too many human beings o
the Earth. In this situation, nature cannot provide enough
food and water for all. Therefore, in order 'to solve' that
problem, **mankind turns to artificially engineered of
producing faster food which changes people's DNA and
causes illness.**

When a test of parental competence, ability, and quality of parents, are not done before pregnancy, the results are as we know it today: ill-fated poor people, sick and violent crooks, prisoners and prostitutes, etc. Such people have reached this situation after a difficult and bitter life journey. In their childhood they mostly had no love, no guiding figure to educate and teach them good manners, respect for others, tolerance, compassion, gentleness, etc. They were educated only for being survival.

Elements of life insights
are provided at home by the parents.
Knowledge and education is provided outside
by the Educational Institutions.

Proper education and training
on the behalf of the governments
would have prevented them to
become a social and economic burden.

Today, this burden uses a huge amounts
From the government's resources
that could have used for science and research.

This produces a considerable regression
in humanity's progress on Earth.

What needs to be done is:

- Only certain couples who are mature emotionally, with financial, physical and intellectual ability, who are compassionate and tolerant, respect others, that have had proper training and education - will receive 'a governmer license' to bring a specific number of children. Such couples can either be a man and a woman, two men or tw women.
  These couples will be given professional support, such as with guidance, advice, practical solutions for family problems, etc.

- In the far future, a worldwide global government will be established. In this way, each one will finally feel as a citizen of a global government with equal global rights.

  The worldwide global government will establish 'childrearing villages', which will offer warmth, love, education, and knowledge.

  Main education will not be in the hands of the biological parents, but rather a global educational staff. The childrer will belong first to their families and second to global government and will enjoy pure love, without belligerence or control. Those children will not have to deal with survival and effects of war. The budgets of government will be devoted to enhancing the welfare of the citizens through the advancement of technology, scientific, medical and genetic research, spiritual communication and spiritual medicine. In addition, 're-education villages' will be established for citizens in need of help.

All human activities have a single purpose
to receive love and recognition.
You have within you - a soul that must receive love.
A lack of love will cause separation and hatred.

ཞ Re-education ᢌ

A child who has had a difficult childhood did not get the attention, love and education protection will often turn his anger and frustration towards himself resulting in self-destruction. **Just like a single match can burn down an entire forest, a single untrained parent can ruin an entire nuclear family and even generation.**

Mistakes committed by parents may ruin an entire childhood and may produce adults that do not respect life and will try to harm the environment by disrespect others, commit crimes, murder, kidnap, etc. The entire society pays for such parental mistakes commit crimes, murder, kidnap, etc. The entire society pays for such parental mistakes throughout continuing generations.

It is not right to think like individuals.
All of society needs to think as one unit.

Governments pay a heavy financial and social price if they focus on rehabilitation rather than promotion and momentum.

Today, governments deal too much with security, terroris
and wars (remember: you cannot die) rather that dealing
with important internal issues such as: education, science,
technology, health, the wellbeing of its citizens, etc.

Instead of denouncing and eliminating all those who failed,
society will learn to accept and guide them and fulfill an
important parental role in their lives, with love and patienc
they will build villages for their re-education, these will
receive a second chance and information about their past w
not be accessible to the general public, they will be
integrated into community service jobs, they will be well
paid for their labor and periodically will receive bonuses fo
persistence, just like children are rewarded, so that they car
make progress. We are all one big united society that must
take care of each other.

❧ Instead of death penalty ❧

As we enter the Aquarian Age, which begins in the year
2106, the frequencies on Earth will become more refined.
People will love more and hate less. When a person kills
another, he does so because his soul is not in a place of
tranquility and peace with himself, he must be taught to
love, understand his mistakes and communicate without
using violence, in villages of re-education.
In cases of taking life of other, the first law (freedom of
choice) is been violated, because the victim's freedom was
revoked in which his life was taken away. Then the second
law (All returns) will come back, as a *karma*, to hunt the
personal life of the offender.

∂ **The United States** ∞

Today half of Earth humanity are life in an age of material and artificial plenty. You can see that in: food, base products, technology, agriculture, entertainment, finance, plastic surgery, etc.

The United States is "the land of unlimited opportunities" Indeed, everything is vast and plentiful in this wonderful country. There is plenty of food, lots of museums, parks and amusement parks and hi-tech industry and gadgets that make life easier. The United States is a global gathering which has increased the wellbeing of the many immigrants who have reached its shores, allowing them to accumulate money & luxuries.

In one hand, United States possesses some of the most advanced scientific and medical technologies but on the other hand a great power of corrupt lobbyists who maintain elites and power mechanisms that are not in the public interest which lead to a high percentage of:

poverty, lack of equal healthcare, selling weapons to all, shooting innocent people, drugs users, racial differences, homelessness, feeding students with junk food while it funded by corporate strengths rather than hot meals, obesity, murder and abductions cases, millions of prisoners which are in private prisons!? And many more.

History

The first ones to invade the United States arrived on ships from Europe, they killed, burned and destroyed Native American villages and often decimated entire populations of

Native Americans and others, who were among the origina inhabitants of America.

These invaders brought slaves to be their laborers, which were dark-skinned Africans who were considered to be inferior because of their appearance and origin and without basic freedom and human rights. These invaders acted toward them with arrogance, meanness, and greediness as everything belonged to them and all must serve them. This attitude continues to secretly exist in our time among various sectors in the United States and many other countries. *The creation* respected and appreciated the enlightened leader Martin Luther King, and sent him to awaken up the 'dark-skinned' people so that they could attain their basic human rights as the rest of the citizens.

Those black slaves have become angry over the years because they are still treated unequally. Let us not forget, that the black man, who is composed of a high percentage o gorillas and a low percentage of extra-terrestrials (alien), does not have a high level of knowledge, but a high level of physical strength.

Even today, many dark-skinned people in the United States feel that they do not belong in America, in spite of their rights and citizenship. This is why they call themselves African Americans, which means that they belong firstly to the continent of Africa and secondly to the United States.

Most African Americans feel frustration as a result of the government discrimination in education, culture, quality of life, housing, and large income differences.

As a minority, their anger and frustration have grown over the years. A high percentage of them are living in ghettos and poor neglected neighborhoods, have their own culture and often higher crime rates.

∂∘ Prisons ∾

It is a mistake to punish 'outlaws' that have broken laws and crossed boundaries (laws that invented by other people) and to remove them from the public eye by placing them in complexes surrounded by fences and guards so that they cannot escape. Humanity does not yet realize that these people are already in their own inner prison. Most of them are the children of 'lost' parents who were not trained to be a good example as parents are should.

The great majority of these prisoners grew up without education, guidance and a lack of love, some of them have become parents themselves to children who resemble them and so it continues, generation after generation.

These prisoner chooses their ways and still the society need to show compassion but not to one who took life. Is difficult to forgive and easy to throw them into prison, as if they were trash, out of sight from the rest of society.

Statistically, a prisoner who is incarcerated mostly does not change his ways. On the contrary, his chances of returning to crime and to prison, again and again, only increase each time he is incarcerated. This is because the prisoners "educate and enrich" one another in prison.

If a prisoner resists re-education and returns to a crime, the his material needs will be taken away from him. The logic behind this: only if you give - then you shall receive. This will continue until he will be re-educated and can serve as a example for others. Remember that all we want is the love and appreciation of the environment.

Approximate statistics about incarceration:

- There is currently estimate figure of 9 million prisoners worldwide.

- The United States has the largest number of prisoners in the world, which estimate about 2.5 million!

  Next in line, as befitting their status as major superpowers are Russia and China.

- Since the 80s', the number of prisoners in the United States has tripled.

- Over 6 million Americans are under 'corrective supervision': one of about every 50 Americans is in jail or on probation.

- African-American citizens comprise about 15 percent of the population in the United States, but comprise about half of the prisoners in the United States!

- About 700 out of every 100,000 white males are incarcerated.

- About 4,500 out of every 100,000 African-American males are incarcerated!

The privatization of prisons in the United States:

How can it be, that "the land of the free" imprisoning more people than any other country in the world?

During the 80s', a process of prison privatization began in the United States. In this process, several corporations were chosen by the government to run the prisons as a profitable business for "saving the country money".

In order to guarantee a profitable income for those corporations, the United States government committed to them the following deal: Each prison will contain a certain quantity of beds, all the prisoners equipment and will active trading unpaid employment which enriches these corporations and the government committed that jails will be about 90% occupied for at least 20 years then penalties must be for long periods.

Thus, the government is committed to supply prisoners to these corporations for filling up the jails and ensure a constant traffic by punishments for every minor transgression.

It is hard to believe that this kind of process is taking place, with a deafening silence by the citizens of the United States, instead of being angry and demonstrate, rebelling and fixing this injustice, which affects all levels of society.

The power to change things will only be by the people, not by the government. This is true for all countries that injustice and tyranny, from ancient times until today. Especially as we march toward the Aquarian Age that

begins in 2106, the signs of the Age have begun, when pow
is turning back to the citizens.

❧ Weapons ❧

The United States is one of the few countries which allow i
citizens to 'protect themselves' by purchasing as many
weapons as they like. This also maintains a thriving corrup
weapons industry.

The creation encourages freedom, but not the freedom to
commit violence. This is also a warning to the government
of the United States of the approach of complete chaos in th
country, which leads to insecurity and fear. That chaos will
arrive as a result of this "limitless weapons freedom.

The result is a situation in which many innocent civilians a
killing, students go on shooting rampages in educational
institutions, citizens hoard weapons in their homes, certain
neighborhoods are not safe to visit, etc.

In the future: Following several years of struggle, the
government will change the law regarding of citizens
possession of carrying weapons which will be allowed only
for those in security-related jobs. The citizens' weapons wil
be collected by the army (with the aid of tanks). This may
create tension and lead to battles between the army and the
citizens and casualties on both sides until the task of
collecting all weapons is complete.

❧ Empires are falling ❧

We are about to enter the Age of Aquarius, in the year 2106. While the 'Rays of Aquarius Age' entered at the year 1638. More details in my second book: The Future.

Today, there are still countries ruled by a tyrannical dictator (North Korea, Syria) and governments (China, Russia) that do not respect the freedom of their citizens.

This type of ruler or governments manages to subdue his citizens with the aid of the army, the police, and collaborators. He denies liberty and freedom of choice to his citizens. The regime rules by taking advantage of their vulnerability, weakness and death threats. The ruler knows that in order to survive, he must rule with an iron fist; otherwise, the citizens will overthrow him.

The ruler knows that he cannot abuse and dominate the people forever and that his time is limited **because the human nature will always fight for freedom.**

Human beings are eternal souls made of divine spirit.

there is nothing to fear! You cannot kill a spirit, then you cannot die!

You must rise up to rebel and initiate revolutions in order to create a new world order for yourselves and for future generations because no one else will do it for you. As part of the civil disobedience, you always must unite with the army forces and police, aid from foreign countries will also be useful.

Civil disobedience

Civil disobedience is the only force that can make a change in the citizens quality life. **The power to change things is in the hands of the people and not the government.**

Governments are fearful of the strength possessed by their citizens. In order to prevent any thought of bringing down the government by the citizens, the governments had established the "internal security". You cannot harass abuse and intimidate people forever. When civil disobedience takes place it is impossible to kill all the citizens of a country!

In every revolution, there will be 'temporary' casualties, that will help achieve the great change for future generations. You cannot die. During a battle, all of the 'temporary' victims will return 'home' to *The creation/ God* and will receive a new body if you wish. You cannot be destroyed, you are an eternal soul that reincarnates in a temporary body again and again.

China

There are over a billion Chinese citizens. Most of them are poor and lacking higher education. The Chinese have always been ruled by a single central government, communist or imperial, which does not allow freedom and full human rights for its citizens. The Chinese nation is indeed the largest on Earth, but it is also the most cowardly nation which does not demonstrate or rebel but however assists the government in maintaining order.

Since the origin of human creation began in Japan and the Chinese were created during the spread of this race, they are the closest to the race of extra-terrestrials (aliens) with robotic thinking, brainwashed and easy to control. The Chinese regime is trying to control the world by increased industrialization in an irresponsible wild madness race while they destroy the resources, especially polluting their own nature reserves and others, such as: water, air, soil, etc. that affect the rest of planet with globalist warming and pollution of natural resources of all humanity.

The Chinese regime is fearful of the strength of its citizens, who might rebel and overthrow it. Therefore, it even not allows their citizens to connect to the worldwide social networks; it enforces many rules and regulations using a vast number of policemen, law enforcers and spies among its citizens. The Chinese citizens should raise and make their own revolution because empires are falling. **The creation will not allow China to continue to destroy Earth!** The Karma always come back to the sender. Nature will 'reply back' and natural disasters likely will occur to happen to every country that is not respecting Earth.

North Korea

Much like the situation in China, most of the citizens of North Korea are poor and can be controlled and brainwashed like extraterrestrials and robots, they are frightened and are withdrawn from the rest of the world so that it would be easy to control them. Their life destiny is to rise up and rebel, with the aid of other countries. This is our duty as a global community to take care of each other, **as we are entering the Aquarius Age, will start in the year 2106. you are welcome to read my book: The Future/2018.** www.lucy4you.com

❧ Summary words ☙

Dear Readers,

Continue to my first book 'Divine Creation',
The theory in this book reveals proofs,
by simple mathematics calculation
of Astro-Numerological order.
The circle of life - has no beginning and no end.

All around is eternal and alive, we can change the states
of matters but never make them disappear.

Please continue to explore
and reach your own truth,
because there never will be a single truth
in order to maintain the Divine Creation engine.

Remember,
The universe always allows free choice
between at least two options
that's why

God can never be One.

1st edition 2016, 2nd edition 2018 © All rights reserved to:

Lucy, Medium

Remote channeling sessions

www.lucy4you.com

CPSIA information can be obtained
at www.ICGtesting.com
Printed in the USA
LVHW030757010621
689025LV00017B/973